**Book 5 of the
Drumshee Timeline Series**

Cora Harrison taught primary-school children for twenty-five years before moving to a small farm in Kilfenora, Co. Clare. The farm includes an Iron Age fort, with the remains of a small castle inside it. The mysterious atmosphere of this ancient place gave Cora the idea for a series of historical novels tracing the survival of the ringfort through the centuries.

Other books in the Drumshee Timeline Series

FAMÍNE SECRET
AT
DRUMSHEE

CORA HARRISON

WOLFHOUND PRESS

Published in 2003 by

WOLFHOUND PRESS
An Imprint of Merlin Publishing
16 Upper Pembroke Street
Dublin 2
Ireland
Tel: +353 1 676 4373
Fax: +353 1 676 4368
publishing@merlin.ie
www.merlin-publishing.com

A CIP catalogue record for this book is available from the British Library.

ISBN 0–86327–916–3

10 9 8 7 6 5 4 3 2 1

Cover Design by Pierce Design
Typeset by Carrigboy Typesetting Services
Printed and bound in Denmark, by Nørhaven Paperback A/S

*For Deirdre McMahon and
Fiona Barry of Inchovea School*

Chapter One

'hew!' said Fiona, as she came out of the cool darkness of the school porch into the bright autumn sun. 'What a smell!'

'Must be your stockings,' said her brother Martin. He was twelve, a year older than Fiona, and never missed an opportunity to annoy his sister.

Fiona tossed back her long blond hair and aimed a blow at his shins with her skipping rope. He dodged around, just out of her reach, calling out in his most teasing voice: 'Fiona's got smelly stockings, smelly stockings, smelly stockings.'

'Don't mind him,' said Deirdre, Fiona's twin. 'He'll soon stop if you take no notice.'

But Fiona did not really mind Martin. On that sunny day in the autumn of 1845, Fiona was happier than she had ever been before. The happiness had been fizzing and bubbling inside her all afternoon, and it was a relief to let it escape.

That morning Mr O'Brien, the landlord, had paid one of his rare visits to the school. He had examined all the children – and Fiona McMahon had shone like a star. No matter what was asked of her, she could do it. She could add, subtract, multiply and divide almost as well as the schoolmaster himself, she could spell every word in the spelling book, and as for reading – well, no one could read like Fiona. When she had read the last passage in the reader without making a single mistake, Mr O'Brien had pulled out of his pocket a book called *Oliver Twist*, by Charles Dickens, which he had bought that morning in Ennis. Fiona had read it so well, with such expression, that the whole schoolroom – from the babies to Mr O'Brien himself – had listened in dead silence for over a quarter of an hour.

The morning had ended with Mr O'Brien promising to call and see Fiona's father, to talk about training her to be a teacher in a couple of years' time. And, best of all, he had given her *Oliver Twist* as a present. At the thought of the beautiful little book, bound in green, lying in her schoolbag, Fiona's happiness bubbled up again and she raced after Martin, breathless and laughing.

Martin, however, had lost interest in teasing Fiona. He was standing by the road, with a puzzled look in his face. There was indeed a terrible smell in the air; and it seemed to be coming from the field across the road – the Big Meadow, the largest field on the McMahons' farm.

Could it be a dead cow? Martin wondered. But no, that was impossible; his father was an excellent farmer who walked his lands every day, he would know where every one of his animals was. In any case, the potatoes were growing in the Big Meadow, and no cow would have been allowed near them. Only that morning John McMahon had said, looking at the potatoes, 'When you all get back from school this afternoon, I think we'll make a start at lifting these fellows. Looks as if we'll get a great crop this year.'

Frowning thoughtfully, Martin crossed the road, followed by the twins and ten-year-old Daniel, the youngest of the family. There was a thick hedge of hawthorn and snowberry between the road and the Big Meadow; when Martin pushed back the thorny branches and looked into the field, what he saw made him freeze in horror.

Without a word to the rest of the family, Martin let go of the branches and started to run down the road, his heavy iron-tipped boots ringing on the stone surface. He turned in at their gate and, hardly slackening his speed, raced up the steep avenue towards their house, shouting at the top of his voice, 'Da, there's something wrong with the potatoes in the Big Meadow!'

Long-legged Fiona raced after him, but Deirdre waited at the gate for plump little Daniel. She looked across the hill to the field where their neighbours, the O'Donoghues, had started to gather in their potatoes; and she felt her heart grow cold.

Instead of putting the potatoes in the baskets, Mr O'Donoghue was throwing them behind him, one by one. His wife sat on the ground with her apron over her head, a picture of despair. The east wind carried their voices towards Deirdre; she could hear Mr O'Donoghue crying, 'Rotten! Every one of them is rotten!'

The next moment, her father rounded the bend in the avenue, carrying his spade, and went into the Big Meadow without a glance at Deirdre.

The potato plants in the meadow, which only that morning had looked so promising in their neat rows of dark green, were black and limp. The stench was overpowering.

John put his foot on the spade and turned over the earth. For a moment no one spoke; then Fiona called out, relief making her voice high and shaky, 'But they're all right! They're beautiful potatoes.'

Deirdre looked at the potatoes; they did look fine. She felt almost sick with relief. Her father lifted the spade again and dug up the next plant. Four big dusty potatoes rolled out of the soil.

'Are they all right, Dad?' asked Martin, looking at the handsome potatoes and the withered, stinking plants with a puzzled air.

John made no answer, but went on to the next plant. This time, in his hurry, he sent the spade right through one of the potatoes – and Martin had his answer. The outside of the potato was good, round and fat and healthy; but that was only the outside. The inside was a putrid, slimy mess.

The four children looked at one another in horror as their father bent down and picked up the potatoes he had already dug. As soon as he touched them, they broke, and the smell was so bad that they all turned their heads away.

At that moment their mother reached the Big Meadow. They looked at her in despair. Nora McMahon was always the one who cheered everyone up, who managed to look on the bright side of things, but now she was silent. As she was coming down the avenue, she, like Deirdre, had seen the O'Donoghues on the hill and had realised that something was badly wrong.

In the end she spoke. Her voice sounded as if she had to force the words out of her throat.

'Can you save anything from them, John?' she asked quietly.

Her husband did not answer. He set to work like a madman, digging out the potatoes, picking them up, smelling them, squeezing them and throwing the rotten ones into the ditch. They all watched in silence, sick with apprehension, afraid to say a word or even offer to help.

After fifteen minutes there were only three or four small potatoes in the basket, and the ditch was filling up with broken potatoes oozing out their creamy corruption.

'What will we eat this winter?' whispered Fiona to Deirdre.

Deirdre said nothing, just shook her head warningly. Fiona began to feel even more frightened. She hated silence – she always liked to talk about everything; but it looked as if no one was going to say anything at all. Her father worked on frantically, digging up the potatoes as if somehow, by sheer speed, he might stop the terrible disease from infecting his family's food for the winter. Her mother just stood there, her face frozen and her arm around Daniel's shoulders. Martin was shifting from one foot to the other, one minute looking as if he was going to offer to help, the next minute thinking better of it; and as for Deirdre – well, of course, thought Fiona crossly, who can ever tell with Deirdre? She always looked the same, no matter what happened. Deirdre kept her feelings to herself.

Their neighbour, Mr Arkins, came into the field. He was big and burly, with the permanently red-brown face of a man who lived most of his life out of doors. Now, however, he suddenly seemed to have shrunk, and his face was a muddy shade of grey.

'I can tell by the stink of them that you have the disease, too,' he said, his voice a broken echo of its normal booming sound. He stood looking helplessly at the foul mess which John had just dug up. Without warning, he lifted his boot and kicked the potatoes over the hedge into the road outside.

'God damn it all,' he screamed, 'how am I going to feed my family this winter? We'll starve, I tell you we'll starve! I've dug up an acre this morning, and even the few potatoes that were whole in the morning have turned black this afternoon. I might as well drown the whole family in the River Fergus right now, and not have to watch them die by inches during the winter.'

The four children watched him in horror, and a whimper of terror came from Daniel. Nora quickly pulled herself together.

7

'Come on, children,' she said quietly. 'Let's get back to the house.'

'But what did he mean?' said Fiona urgently, as they went up the avenue. 'He can't drown all his children. What a terrible thing to say! And he's got the sweetest little baby –'

'Don't think about him,' answered her mother. 'It may not be as bad as they think. You know the way it is with men – they're always making a fuss. Let's get something to eat, and then everyone will feel better.'

'Yes, but what are we going to do?' insisted Fiona. 'If we can't eat potatoes, what will we eat?'

'Well, we're a lot better off than most people,' said Nora. 'Your father had a very good crop of oats this year, so we can have plenty of porridge. We have plenty of milk, the hay crop was good – that will keep the cows and the horse going, so we won't need to use the oats for them – the hens are laying well, and when January comes we'll get eggs from the ducks. We've got the meat from the pig all salted, and if needs be we can kill a calf. We won't starve. It will be a hard winter for us, but I'm afraid it will be a much worse one for our neighbours. Remember, we have twenty acres; most of the other families around here are lucky if they have a single acre to feed themselves.'

Fiona nodded and fell back behind her mother to wait for Deirdre, who was standing looking across the hill.

'Deirdre,' she said. 'Don't tell Ma or Da about what Mr O'Brien said, or about my prize. It will be spoilt if I tell it now, while everyone's thinking about potatoes.'

'All right,' said Deirdre. The twins were very different, in looks and in every other way. At that moment, Deirdre had as many worries in her mind as Fiona did, but she preferred to keep them to herself and think about them. Their mother always said that when the twins were born, God must have run short of tongues, so he only had one for the two of them – and Fiona had the one.

'You'd better tell Martin not to say anything either,' Deirdre added, and the two girls turned to wait for their brother.

'Martin,' said Fiona, as he came up the hill towards them, 'Martin, don't say anything at home about my prize, will you? I'll tell them about it another time.'

'The last thing I was thinking about,' said Martin, grinding the words out furiously, 'was you and your stupid prize. Trust you to be thinking about yourself. I suppose you're afraid that there might not be enough fuss over you if people were thinking about starving this winter.'

With that he went on up the hill, kicking the gravel, his head down, his shoulders hunched, the picture of misery.

Fiona glared after him. 'He's mean and stupid too,' she said bitterly. 'I'm not just thinking of myself. I just thought it would be the wrong time to mention it.'

'Here's Da,' said Deirdre. 'I think you should tell him. You know how much he thinks of school and book-learning. If you tell him now, he'll have something else to think about tonight, instead of just worrying about the potatoes.'

Fiona flushed crimson with shame. Martin was right, she admitted to herself. She did not really want her moment of triumph spoiled.

She struggled with herself for a few seconds, and then ran to meet her father.

'Da,' she said shyly, 'I got a prize in school today from Mr O'Brien. It's a book called *Oliver Twist*, by Mr Charles Dickens. Mr O'Brien is going to come and see you about me becoming a teacher.'

Deirdre was right: John and Nora McMahon's delight in their clever daughter helped to cheer up the house a little. Nevertheless, it was sad and subdued family that sat around the turf fire that evening. And while Fiona, in the little loft bedroom which she shared with Deirdre, wept over the miseries of Oliver Twist in the workshop, her mother and father, with heavy hearts, spoke in low voices about the hard winter ahead.

Chapter Two

It was a bad winter for everyone. John was haunted by the fear that the same disease might attack the potatoes next year, so he threw himself into the back-breaking work of digging the heavy clay soil in the Togher Field, so that he could plant an extra five acres of oats the next spring. Nora spent hours scouring the hedgerows and the edges of fields, looking for green sorrel to keep the family healthy.

Martin, to his great delight, was allowed to leave school in order to help his father, but Daniel and the twins continued to go. John did not know how long he could afford the pennies for school – he was short of money this year, as he had no potatoes to sell – but he was determined that Fiona, at least, would have as much education as she needed in order to become a teacher. It wouldn't matter so much about Deirdre, John thought; she'd probably be happier at home with her mother, sewing or knitting. And Daniel would love to leave school and join his brother on the farm. Fiona, however, was different. Come what might, he would have to scrape together the money to give Fiona the education which she so passionately wanted.

By the middle of November the school was three quarters empty. Very few families could afford a penny a week; and in the struggle for life that was going on in most houses, book-learning was not considered to be of much importance. To Fiona's dismay, there was talk of closing the school at Christmas.

She worked desperately hard, cramming her mind with every bit of information the schoolmaster possessed, repeating every piece of poetry over and over again, practising sums in her head even after she and Deirdre had gone to bed, and writing long stories in a copybook which her father had bought her in Ennis. Daniel faithfully braved the gander in order to collect goose quills to make pens for her; in reward, Fiona would take him down to the underground storeroom in the old fort behind the farmhouse and read him the latest pages of her story. As she sat there, reading her neat copperplate handwriting and watching Daniel's eyes shining with excitement in the light of the candle, Fiona began to feel that she did not want to be a teacher any more. Now she knew what she really wanted to do: she would be a writer, just like Mr Charles Dickens.

Fiona needed to live in her imagination just then, because the real world was so unpleasant. Everywhere she went, she saw thin pale faces and skeletal bodies. Even home was no longer the pleasant, happy place which it had once been. Her father and mother were hardly speaking to each other. Nora wanted to help feed the neighbours, but John would not hear of it.

'We have only enough for ourselves,' he said angrily. 'If you give food away, then it's our children who'll go hungry. Remember, there won't be any more potatoes until August or September. We have eight months to go.'

Every day John went down to the storeroom, carefully checking that no outsider could see where he went, and stores turnips, oats, honey and goats' cheeses there. Every night he carefully locked up the cows and the calves so that no one could steal them.

'Watch them all the time, Martin,' he warned. 'A man from Corofin told me his cattle died of weakness because people were coming at night and drawing pints of blood out of them. You'd never know – the hunger might have them trying it even in the middle of the day.'

One day, in the middle of December, the school-master told the children that the school would be closed from that day onwards. There were too few children left to make it worthwhile; and in any case, disease was spreading through the countryside.

The three McMahon children walked home quietly. For Deirdre and Daniel, it was the end of their child-hood; but for Fiona it was a tragedy.

'Never mind,' said Deirdre. 'You'll be able to practise your lessons at home. After all, by now you probably know as much as the schoolmaster does. Yesterday, you were right and he was wrong in that sum you were doing.'

'He was going to teach me Latin,' said Fiona bitterly,' and now I'll never learn it.'

Deirdre did not answer. Fiona lifter her head and looked at her crossly, glad of an opportunity to quarrel with someone; but to her surprise, Deirdre was not looking at her. She was looking across the hill, at the figure of their mother, wrapped in a shawl and carrying a basket, crossing the Rough Field.

'Where's she going?' said Fiona, distracted from her sorrows for a moment.

'I think she's bringing food to the Arkins family,' whispered Deirdre.

'I hope Da doesn't see her,' Fiona whispered back. 'He told her not to. I don't know why he's so mean. We can spare a little food for them. After all, they're our nearest neighbours.'

'Tommy Arkins is sick, too,' added Daniel. 'He'll need food to get him better.'

The two girls looked at each other apprehensively.

'I hope Ma doesn't pick up any fever,' said Deirdre in a low voice.

'Oh, she won't,' said Fiona. 'Ma's never sick, she never catches anything.'

'Don't say that,' said Deirdre quickly. 'It's not lucky.'

The next day, Deirdre was sitting at the window sewing, and Fiona, at the kitchen table, was absent-mindedly stroking the silky smoothness of her feather pen as she thought out the next exciting episode of her story. A sudden crash, and the hiss of boiling water on hot sods of turf, made them both jump up in alarm.

The big iron pot of water had slipped from their mother's hands. She was leaning against the stone chimney, with her hand pressed to her forehead and her face as white as the limewashed walls. She turned to look at the twins, her eyes misty and feverish. With a last spurt of strength, she gasped: 'Don't come near. Call your father – I think I have the fever.'

Fiona screamed, and then pressed her hands to her mouth in a frantic attempt at self-control. Deirdre slipped out of the door without a word.

Fiona took several deep breaths.

'Move away from the fire, Ma,' she said urgently. 'Your dress is near the flames. Don't worry, I won't come near you. Deirdre has gone for Da.'

It took Deirdre five minutes to find their father, and those were the longest five minutes of Fiona's life. She stood on one side of the kitchen, watching Nora, who had sunk down in a heap on the floor, moaning quietly. Fiona hated herself: she wanted to go to her mother, lift her head, give her a drink, but a paralysing fear overcame her. She could see dark blotches swelling on her mother's ankles, and she knew that those were a sign of the dreaded black fever.

She closed her eyes, like a small child, willing the blotches to disappear; but when she opened them she could see that the swellings were getting worse. It seemed impossible, but her mother – who only a quarter of an hour before had been able to move about getting the evening meal – was very sick indeed.

Fiona took two hesitating steps forward, but some instinct made Nora open her eyes. In a hoarse, almost unrecognisable voice, she said, 'Fiona, keep back, I tell you!'

Fiona drew back. I have to do what I'm told, she argues with herself.

The kitchen was getting dark. The light from the glowing sods of turf was reflected in the plates on the dresser; the sides of bacon hanging from the rafters cast swaying shadows; and the cattle outside were lowing on their nightly journey to their cabins.

The door burst open and John ran in, followed by Martin and Deirdre and Daniel. He took one glance at his wife, lying on the kitchen floor, and his face darkened. He looked angry and frightened at the same time.

'Get outside, all of you,' he shouted at the children. 'Get outside and stay outside!'

The four children stood outside the cottage and looked at one another. Their lips were white. Fiona felt as if she were about to get sick.

'Let's do the milking,' said Martin abruptly. 'Will you help me, Deirdre?'

'I'll shut the hens in,' said Daniel.

'You do the ducks, Fiona,' said Deirdre. She knew that Fiona was on the point of fainting, but it was better to give her something to do than to leave her standing there, trying to hope while knowing that there was no hope. And the ducks were always such a nuisance to get into their house in the evening, sailing around and around their pond as if determined to cling to the safety of the water, that you really had to put your mind to the job.

So Martin and Deirdre did the milking, and Daniel shut the hens in their house, and Fiona eventually managed to round up the ducks. And then there was nothing to do but stand and wait. It was getting dark and a few stars were appearing in the sky, but still the four children stood outside the door – not speaking to one another, just standing there.

Finally their father appeared. He opened the two halves of the door and lugged out the hay-bag which usually lay on the children's bedsteads.

'Take these to the storeroom,' he ordered. 'I don't want any of you in the house until your mother is better. Martin, in the morning you take the horse and ride into Kilferora, and get a bottle of fever mixture from the doctor at the dispensary. You'll have to sort out the work of looking after the animals between you. I'll hand you the pot and you can cook porridge in the old cabin over there. Don't forget to have an egg and some milk every day. You won't go hungry. Leave some milk at the door for me and your mother, and some porridge, too. But remember, you must not come into the house again until I tell you.'

Chapter Three

It was a beautiful day in April 1846. The weather, as so often happens in the west of Ireland, was better than in the middle of the summer. The sun shone, the fields were covered with white and yellow flowers, and the birds sang in the hedges. The newly-limewashed walls of the small cottage at Drumshee shone in the sunshine.

Martin had painted them only a week ago, in an effort to show the landlord that he would be able to take the place of his dead father, able to farm the holding, able to take care of his sisters and brother; but it had been a wasted effort. Tomorrow the four children were to be taken to the workhouse.

Perhaps it's for the best, thought Martin. The potato crop had failed the year before and might fail again. If his father and mother had been alive they might have managed, by growing extra oats and selling some cattle. But Martin was only thirteen, and Daniel only eleven; and Deirdre and Fiona had never done much around the farm. Fiona was always reading or writing stories, and Deirdre was always doing house-work or needlework.

Martin looked at the four cows in the cow cabin, the horse in his stable, the pig in the pigsty, and shrugged his shoulders. No doubt the landlord would take all of the animals to pay the rent.

'Martin,' said Fiona, as he went into the cottage. 'Martin, do we have to go the workhouse? I think I'll die if we do! In my book about Oliver Twist it said that they starved and beat the children in the workhouse. I can't bear the thought of it! Let's run away and hide in the bog!'

Martin looked at her and sighed with exasperation. She's always living in the clouds, he thought. 'Don't be stupid, you've known for days that we have to go,' he said shortly, and turned away so he would not see the tears spilling out of her eyes for the twentieth time that day.

Deirdre put an arm around her sister. That was typical of the twins: no matter how much they fought, they always stood up for each other against the rest of the world. Just now, Deirdre was hating Martin furiously. Why can't he leave Fiona alone? she thought. Of all the family, Fiona was the most upset. When their father and mother had been alive Fiona had been trained as a teacher; now her world had ended. Deirdre looked with pity at the sensitive pale face, blotched by constant tears; the brown eyes with dark circles around them; and the long blond hair, which had been her mother's delight, hanging limp and neglected around Fiona's face.

Martin avoided Deirdre's reproachful glance and turned to look out over the half-door.

'Would you believe it!' he said. 'Just look at that.'

Daniel joined him at the door.

'Why, it's Higglety!' he said joyfully. 'Come and see, Fiona – she has eight lovely little chicks with her. Aren't they early this year?'

'Just in time to make eight lovely dinners for the landlord,' said Martin sourly.

Higglety was a black hen; every year, she went away by herself and came back with a clutch of chicks. No matter how much the children hunted, they never could find out where she went, so there was always great excitement when she returned. Even now, Fiona dried her eyes and joined her brothers at the door with a faint smile on her lips.

It was only Deirdre who began to understand the meaning behind Martin's words. She looked at him questioningly.

'Oh yes,' he said harshly. 'Everything we own will go to the landlord, to pay the rent we owe him.'

Fiona's eyes widened with horror. 'Let's not allow him! We'll hide everything. We're coming back, aren't we, as soon as we can?'

Martin groaned. 'We're not in one of your stories, Fiona. How on earth - ?' He caught a warning glance from Deirdre and subsided; he didn't really want to start Fiona crying again. And he could see that Deirdre was thinking hard. Deirdre did very little talking, but when she did speak, she usually talked sense. Martin prepared to listen.

'I think we should think about coming back,' Deirdre began, slowly and hesitantly. 'It will give us something to hope for. I have an idea that we might be allowed when we're fourteen, but it might be before that. Anyway, we must stay in touch with each other. Daniel, you'll be with Martin — he'll look after you — and Fiona and I will be together. We'll try to speak to one of you boys every day. And we'll never forget that we are one family.'

'What about hiding things, then?' asked Daniel. 'Where will we do that?'

Martin looked at him in despair. 'Daniel, we won't be back for years.' Or never, he added silently in his own mind. 'How can we hide the cows and the horse and tell them to wait quietly until we get back?'

'No, but we can hide things like the pots and the spinning wheel and father's traps, and maybe even the stools and the beds,' said Deirdre. 'And I know where we can put them. We'll put them in the storeroom!'

The children looked at one another with dawning excitement. The storeroom was known only to their own family, and it had always been impressed upon them that it had to be kept a secret. Their father had told them that it had always been a secret, even when he was a boy. No one else in the neighbourhood knew about it.

So that last evening at Drumshee, which could have been such an agonisingly sorrowful time, turned out to be quite exciting and hopeful. The children made journey after journey from the little house up to the *cathair*, the fort on top of the hill. Martin had moved the heavy flagstone which covered the entrance. He had been careful not to damage the grasses which grew over it; when it was put back, no one would ever guess that anything lay beneath.

Already in the storeroom were the ancient jars where the oats had been stored, the seed corn that John McMahon had not lived to sow. Martin felt his eyes prick with tears at the sight, but he hurriedly put down the table which he was carrying and went back to help Daniel dismantle the iron bedsteads.

Fiona even took down her schoolbooks and her precious *Oliver Twist*. Martin said nothing, though he wondered how they would last in the damp. Instead he turned his attention to his father's tools.

'Anything that's made of iron will rust,' he said to Daniel, who was following him, 'so we must grease the shovel and the spade and all the tools; then we'll wrap them in rags and hang them on the wall, so there's a chance they'll survive. Hang up, Da's beekeeping hat and veil, too, and the hay-bags.'

'I'm going to put some big branches in front of the entrance to the cart-house,' said Fiona, who was filled with a kind of restless gaiety. 'Then the landlord's agent will never see the cart. At least that will still be there when we come back, even if we don't have the horse.'

The two boys grinned at each other, but neither said a word. Who knows, she might even be right, thought Martin. After all, theirs was a substantial farm, not like the poor cabins with half an acre that were being pulled down every day. The landlord would probably hope to let the farm; but what with the deaths from famine and disease, and the numbers of people leaving the country every day, not many people would want a farm in the west of Ireland.

A little warm feeling of hope began to grow inside Martin's heart. Perhaps the McMahons *would* be able to come back . . .

He turned back to the work of greasing the tools with new energy. When he was finished, he even helped Fiona to make a wax seal from a melted candle, to put around the box which held her books.

Chapter Four

t was after midnight when the children finished their storage work, so they were all tired and sleepy when the landlord's agent and his men arrived the next morning. They watched silently as the rough-looking men drove away the horse and the four brown cows. The men were less successful with the Billy goat and his four wives. Billy kicked the agent hard in the knee; then, followed by the other goats, he jumped the hedge and took off across the fields. Higglety and her brood of chick were nowhere to be seen; and the ducks, including Fiona's pet, Spooky, simply flew away, circling overhead and then following the river down the valley towards Lough Fergus.

The children's eyes followed the ducks until they disappeared. Then they turned and silently got into the cart. Fiona kept her head in her hands, desperately trying to choke down her sobs, while the other three sat in stony silence gazing at the little white-washed house.

It took an hour and a half, over the rough roads, to reach the workhouse. By the time they arrived, the four children were exhausted and shaking with nervousness.

They climbed down from the cart and timidly entered the receiving house. Here they were separated: Martin and Daniel were taken to the boys' section and Deirdre and Fiona to the girls' house.

The porteress took the two girls to the bathhouse, which was a small whitewashed room with a blazing furnace; in the centre of it was a large bath, its steaming water clouded with carbolic soap. To the twins' horror, they were immediately stripped of their clothes and their hairs was cut short, clipped close to the scalp. All their clothes were thrown into a large furnace.

At the sight, Fiona's temper blazed.

'There's no need to do that,' she said hotly. 'My sister and I don't have lice or disease!'

'It's the rule,' said the porteress, in an expressionless voice. Gathering up Fiona's heavy blond locks of hair, she threw them into the fire as well.

The room was filled with the acrid smell of burning cloth and sizzling hair. Fiona began to choke, and then to cough. Deirdre looked at her in a worried way. When Fiona was young she had suffered badly from asthma, but there had been no problems with it for a long time. Deirdre prayed that her sister would be able to control her breathing. Already the porteress was looking at her suspiciously. If Fiona was made to go into the infirmary, she would surely pick up some awful fever.

'Get into the bath, Fiona,' Deirdre said in a low voice. 'The hot water will help your chest.'

Turning to the porteress, she added politely, 'Shall I help you?' Without waiting for an answer, she picked up her own curly brown hair and threw it into the fire.

It was funny, but she felt nothing when she did that – no sorrow, no regret. Long nicely-combed hair and good woollen clothes were things of the past; and it's no good looking back into the past, Deirdre thought as she climbed into the strong-smelling water beside her sister. The only thing to do was to be as polite and helpful as possible to everyone, give no one any trouble, and hope that they would survive the next few days. After all, they were lucky to be alive; they could have died of the dreaded black fever which had killed their father and mother, or of starvation, like many of their neighbours.

When the porteress was satisfied that both girls were clean, she left the room and returned with two skimpy cotton dresses and two petticoats of linsey-woolsey. Fiona winced when she felt the harsh, scratchy material against her skin. Deirdre hardly noticed. She busied herself tying laces and doing up buttons for her sister, praying that Fiona would keep hold of her temper and that they would get through the day with no problems.

'There, now,' said the porteress when they were dressed. 'Now you look like two nice clean girls.'

'We were perfectly clean before, and we smelt a lot nicer before that foul carbolic bath,' retorted Fiona, getting the angry words out before Deirdre could stop her.

The porteress looked at her sourly. 'You'll change you tune before the week is out, my lady,' she said. 'You'll have to learn that you're in the workhouse now. You're an orphan and you're dependent on charity. If Matron hears you speak like that, you'll be out on the side of the road. Plenty have died there during the last few years. Think yourself lucky.'

'Deirdre,' said Fiona in a whisper, as they followed the porteress across the yard, 'I wish we had died. Why didn't we? It would have been much better . . .'

'Ssh,' said Deirdre crossly. We didn't die, she thought, because our Ma and Da gave their lives to keep us well.

She thought back to that terrible morning when they had found the cottage empty and a newly-dug grave under the old ash tree, next to St Bridget's shrine. They had searched for days for their sick father, but in the end they knew that he had left Drumshee while he still had enough strength; had left before he could infect any of his children; had given up his life so that they might be saved.

And I'm not going to allow our lives to be wasted, thought Deirdre. I must keep Fiona happy and make her see sense, and I must keep in contact with Martin and Daniel.

She straightened her shoulders and, holding her head high, followed the porteress into Matron's room.

Matron was a short, fat woman with cold grey eyes. Many a starving person, entering the workhouse, must have looked at her plumpness with disbelief and perhaps with a measure of hope. However, any belief that they had come to the land of plenty would have died when they looked into these merciless eyes, grey as the stone on the Burren and just as hard. There were two kinds of people in Deborah Smith's world: the kind who had money and possessions, and the kind who had nothing. She regarded the second group as less valuable than the animals in the fields; she wasted no sympathy on them, and gave them just enough food to keep them alive.

She looked at the two girls with a sharp, measuring glance.

'How old?' she said abruptly.

'We're both twelve, Ma'am,' said Deirdre softly. 'We're twins.'

'Have you been to school?'

'Yes, Ma'am,' replied Deirdre.

'What book?'

'Sixth book, Ma'am.'

Matron looked up with slight surprise on her face. They did not often get children who had been to school, and they had certainly never had anyone as advanced as this. She wondered whether the girl was lying, but a glance at the calm, open face in front of her removed her suspicions.

'Well, in that case,' she said, 'there's certainly no need for you to attend the school here. You've learned enough.'

'Oh, but please,' stammered Fiona, 'please may I continue at school? I was getting on very well, and my father promised that I could be a teacher.'

Matron gave a short laugh. 'Well, what you or your father wanted is nothing to do with us here. We've got a teacher and we don't want another. You can learn something useful.' She turned to the porteress. 'Take them to the sewing room. They can learn to spin.'

Deirdre grabbed Fiona's hand and gave it a comforting squeeze. She bobbed a curtsey in the direction of Matron, and then followed the porteress down the echoing stone corridor.

Chapter Five

The sewing room was long and cold, with a high arched ceiling and a stone floor. At one end was a big loom where several women were weaving cloth, passing shuttles wound with wool in and out of the cross-threads. Along the side of the room were a few spinning wheels, which made a busy humming sound as the raw wool was spun into hanks, ready for the weavers or the knitters. In the centre of the room were some long tables where petticoats and dresses were being cut out and sewn together. Several girls were knitting. Everywhere there was almost complete silence and an atmosphere of depression and despair.

The porteress took Deirdre and Fiona over to one of the women who were spinning.

'Matron says these two girls must learn to spin,' she said. 'That's a cheeky one,' she added, pointing at Fiona. 'Make sure you make her work.' With a glare around the room to make sure that everyone was working, the porteress stalked out, the iron tips on her stiff leather shoes almost striking sparks on the stone floor.

'Don't mind her,' said the woman in a whisper. 'I'm Old Sally. I'll look after you. You look too young to be here. You should be at school, but I suppose they thought they could make some money out of you.'

Deirdre smiled timidly at the woman. She was quite old, with white hair, and she looked kind. Deirdre wondered whether she could tell her that they could already spin – their mother had taught them a few years before. She decided to say nothing; it was probably safest to say as little as possible. In any case, it would be hard to say that Fiona could really spin. She never touched the spinning wheel if she could help it, and Deirdre and Nora had grown so tired of helping her to mend her thread that they had fallen into the habit of doing all the spinning themselves.

'Now,' said Old Sally, 'you sit here, one on each side of me, and I'll show you how to do it. You're lucky girls to start off with the spinning. Most of the girls start off with knitting, and even then they're usually older than you.'

'I don't really want to learn to spin,' began Fiona, but Deirdre nudged her hard and she stopped.

'Well, we'll let your sister try first,' said Old Sally kindly. 'What's your name, my dear?'

'I'm Deirdre and my sister is Fiona. We're twins.'

Deirdre sat beside Old Sally and listened to the instructions with her usual careful attention. Then she began, twisting the wool in one hand and turning the spinning wheel with the other. Slowly and carefully she worked; she was very out of practice, as she had done no spinning since the terrible time when her mother and father fell sick, but after about ten minutes her old skill came back to her. Old Sally was delighted.

'Well, you're going to be a treasure to me,' she whispered. 'My hands are getting very stiff with rheumatics, and I was afraid they'd put me working in the infirmary. But if you help me, I might last a while longer.'

'I think I'd prefer working in the infirmary to spinning,' said Fiona in a low voice to Deirdre.

'Oh, don't say that, pet,' said Old Sally in alarm. 'The ones who go nursing in the infirmary always end up getting fever themselves. It's the worst job in the whole place.'

After watching Deirdre work for about half an hour, Old Sally insisted that Fiona should try her hand at the spinning wheel. However, Fiona made so many mistakes, tangling up the spinning wheel and breaking the wool so often, then Old Sally was only too glad to allow her to hand the wheel over to Deirdre again.

'Just watch your sister and you'll soon get the idea of it,' she said kindly.

Fiona watched for a while, but she soon got bored and began a long story in her head. She imagined that they had a very rich relation, over in America, who would come and take them all out of the working-house. She imagined him stepping onto the deck of a ship in America, with a servant carrying a trunk full of beautiful clothes and books, all presents for the McMahon children; she imagined him arriving at the workhouse, and in her mind she was just taking dignified leave of Matron when a hard hand came down on her shoulder and twisted her around towards the spinning wheel.

'Aren't you supposed to be learning to spin, girl?' hissed Matron's harsh voice. 'Your sister is doing well; now let's see what you can do.'

Deirdre sat in agony while Fiona, who was upset and angry at being abruptly dragged from her dreams, made the worst possible attempt at spinning. Still, she reminded herself, it was supposed to be their first time, so perhaps Matron would not be too angry. She was right in that: Matron was so pleased at how well Deirdre seemed to have learned that she suspected that Old Sally had spent almost all the time with the more promising of the twins.

'See that you teach Fiona as well as Deirdre, Sally,' she warned. 'That was disgraceful. She'll have to do better than that.'

With that, Matron stalked out of the room.

Old Sally, however, had herself to think about, and she knew that she would only be allowed to stay in the sewing room as long as she could produce plenty of well-spun wool. For most of the afternoon, she kept Deirdre hard at work at the spinning wheel, while Fiona, sitting beside her, went happily on with the story in her head. Only when the door started to open did Old Sally quickly indicate to Fiona to take Deirdre's place. This time, when Matron came over, it looked as if Fiona had just spun a nice, even hank of wool; and Matron gave a satisfied nod.

In any case, Matron had another matter on her mind. With her was a tall, well-dressed young lady who was carrying a beautiful piece of exquisitely-stitched lace. Matron strode to the centre of the room and clapped her hands for silence. The low murmur immediately died down; you could have heard a pin drop in the silence that followed.

'Now listen to me, women,' said Matron abruptly. 'The guardians of this workhouse have appointed Miss Mary O'Connell to teach lacemaking to six women here. It is a great skill to have; people pay large sums of money for even small pieces of lace. It will be a useful thing to be able to do when you leave the workhouse, and while you are here the lace can be sold to buy food for you all. Miss O'Connell, would you like to look at the sewing-women? You can decide which ones seem good enough for you to teach.'

Deirdre's eyes followed the elegant figure of Miss O'Connell with great longing. I wish I could learn to make lace, she thought. When Matron went to the other end of the room, Deirdre quietly got to her feet and tiptoed across to the table where Miss O'Connell was showing the sewing-women the beautiful piece of lace.

'The pattern is made by stitching these pieces of fine cambric onto the net,' Miss O'Connell was saying. 'Then, when the pattern is right, you cut away the leftover pieces of cambric, and if you like you can join up the parts of the pattern with bars of stitching.'

At that stage, Deirdre saw Old Sally making urgent signs for her to come back and take over the spinning wheel again, before Fiona made too great a mess of the work. She sighed to herself, but hurried back obediently and sorted out the thread. By the time Matron returned, she had the wheel working smoothly again.

Miss O'Connell, however, had noticed Deirdre's interest. She walked over and watched her for a few minutes.

'This girl has only just learned to spin this afternoon,' boasted Old Sally. 'Isn't she getting on very well?'

'Really!' Miss O'Connell was obviously impressed. Deirdre could feel her face getting hot. She prayed that Fiona would say nothing – but, luckily, Fiona wasn't really listening. She had got to the place in her story where her rich relation was asking her whether she would prefer to be a teacher, or to go to London and be presented to the young Queen Victoria.

Miss O'Connell addressed Deirdre. 'Are you able to sew, my dear?'

'Yes, Ma'am.' Deirdre's cheeks were still scarlet.

Miss O'Connell went over to Matron and spoke to her in a low voice. Deirdre could just hear her saying something about 'the younger the better'. Then Matron beckoned her over.

'Let's see you sew, then,' she said shortly.

One of the women handed Deirdre the handkerchief that she was hemming, and Deirdre took it up with trembling hands. She sat still for a moment, with Matron's words echoing in her ears: 'people pay large sums of money for even small pieces of lace . . .' Perhaps this is my big chance, Deirdre thought.

She drew in a deep breath; then, with suddenly steady hands, she began to stitch. Taking the greatest care, she sewed with tiny, almost invisible stitches. Behind her back, Matron and Miss O'Connell exchanged glances.

Before five minutes had passed, Deirdre had finished the handkerchief. She held it out silently to Matron. She dared not even look at Miss O'Connell.

Matron signalled to Deirdre to return to Old Sally. Fiona squeezed her sister's hand. She wasn't very interested in all this sewing, but she felt that in the last few minutes something important had happened for Deirdre.

Matron was taking her visitor away. Deirdre wanted desperately to ask whether she might be good enough to learn lacemaking, but she didn't dare do anything to annoy Matron. None of the sewing-women asked anything either; but Deirdre could see that Kitty, the woman whose handkerchief she had finished, was looking at her with angry dislike.

Deirdre bent her head over the spinning wheel; but she looked up again, with a little bit of hope in her heart, as she realised that Miss O'Connell was trying to catch her eye. As soon as Deirdre looked at her, Miss O'Connell gave her a reassuring smile. Deirdre began to hope for the best.

'You see, Fiona,' she said that night, when they were in the bed which they shared in the long bleak dormitory, 'you see, if I could become a lacemaker, I'd be able to earn some money to buy us food when we go back to Drumshee. And when Martin gets the farm going again, we might be able to afford to have you train as a teacher. Then we'd be quite rich.'

The two girls hugged each other. Fiona did have some worries about how she would manage the spinning, without Deirdre to help her, but she put them out of her head in her usual way – by going on with her stories in her mind. She had decided to tell her rich relation that she would go to the court and be presented to Queen Victoria first, before becoming a teacher.

And so they both fell asleep – Deirdre dreaming of an exquisite piece of lace which she had made all by herself, and Fiona dreaming of silks and velvets at the court of Queen Victoria.

Chapter Six

The next day was Sunday, and after a better breakfast than usual, everyone went to church. The church was a small stone building at the back of the workhouse. Originally it had been built to hold all the people who lived in the workhouse, but now there was such overcrowding that there had to be two services. The first service of the morning was for the children – boys on one side of the church, girls on the other.

When Deirdre and Fiona came into the church, they looked eagerly along the rows of boys until they saw two familiar dark curly heads. Martin and Daniel were together. Deirdre guessed that might mean that they were in the same dormitory, perhaps even in the same bed. She hoped so: she knew that Daniel often had nightmares, and it would be a comfort to him to have Martin there.

'How are we going to talk to them?' whispered Fiona.

'We'll wait for them outside the church if we can. Otherwise we'll have to ask Matron for permission.'

'You'll have to ask her, then. She hates me.'

Deirdre froze with horror as she saw Matron look around to see where the sound was coming from. She pinched Fiona hard to make her be quiet. Fiona scowled. When I'm a rich young lady, she thought, I'll get my own back on that Matron.

When the service was over, the boys went out first; by the time the girls came out, there was no sign of Martin and Daniel. Deirdre and Fiona dawdled outside the church for as long as they dared, and finally set off down the hedge-lined path towards the girls' house. Deirdre was trying to build up her courage to go to Matron's office when they were startled by a low hiss from the other side of the hedge.

'Just stand still for a moment,' came Martin's voice in a low whisper. 'Fiona, bend down and pretend to be buttoning up your shoe.'

'Oh, Martin,' whispered Deirdre. 'How are you both?'

'We're all right,' said Martin. 'How are you two managing?'

'We're learning to spin, and I might have a chance to learn to make lace.'

'I can imagine how much Fiona's enjoying the spinning,' said Martin with a low chuckle.

Fiona's heart lightened a little. It was like old days to have Martin teasing her. From her position on the path she could see two pairs of black boots under the hedge.

'How's Daniel?' she asked anxiously.

'He's all right. He's going to school, and I'm working in the garden growing vegetables. I planted four hundred turnip seeds yesterday.'

'We mustn't stay here for too long – someone will see us,' said Deirdre hurriedly. 'Let's meet here every evening at five o'clock exactly. That's when we're allowed out for some fresh air, and you two will just be going back indoors.'

'We'll do our best. We'd better go now.'

Deirdre looked very happy on the way back to the girls' house, but Fiona was conscious of a slight feeling of uneasiness. Something felt wrong, somehow.

It was only while she was trying to swallow the disgusting mess of watery soup and rice that was supposed to be Sunday dinner that it suddenly came into her head. Daniel had not said a word, all the time that they were together. He hadn't even bent down to look under the hedge to see her. Is Daniel really all right? she wondered. It's not like him to be silent.

Throughout the whole of that long, dull Sunday afternoon, Fiona worried about Daniel. They were not allowed to do anything on Sundays, not even go for a walk. Deirdre sat with her hands folded and her eyes blank, but Fiona knew she was thinking about lace-making, going over and over in her mind how to do it. Deirdre was like that; she loved making things.

Fiona wandered around restlessly, and finally gathered a group of girls and began to tell them the story of *Oliver Twist*. Unfortunately, when she came to the sad bit of the story, where poor little Oliver was beaten for asking for some more food in the workhouse, several of the girls started to cry. Matron, came bustling up to find out what the matter was, and the day ended with disgrace for Fiona, who had been labelled in Matron's mind as a troublemaker.

The next morning, as soon as they had eaten their watery porridge, the twins followed the women into the sewing room. They could see instantly that there had been a change. In front of the window there was a new table, covered in a white cloth, and in front of it were six chairs. On the back of each chair was a spotless white pinafore. On the table, in front of each chair, were pieces of net with patterns traced on them and pieces of fine white cambric.

A tremor of excitement ran through the room. Who was going to be chosen for the lacemaking? The women knew well that any money they earned would be kept by the guardians of the workhouse; but still, most of them longed for a change and nearly all of them hoped desperately that somehow they would be able to get out of the workhouse when the terrible famine was over.

One by one, Matron called over five women. Each one put on a white apron, so that no stain or smudge could dirty their work. They sat at the table and waited while Matron had a whispered conversation with Miss O'Connell.

Deirdre sat in an agony of apprehension. Had she only imagined the encouraging smile which Miss O'Connell had given her on Saturday?

Finally, Kitty was called over. Deirdre bent her head, and tears pricked at her eyes. But after a short conversation with Miss O'Connell, Kitty was sent back again, and Matron was beckoning to Deirdre.

'Miss O'Connell imagines that you might be easily trained for lacemaking,' she said sourly. 'I'm afraid I don't agree. I think you are too young. However, the Board of Guardians has given her the power to make the choice. But I have insisted that you shall have only a week's trial. If, after that time, you do not show yourself to be as good as the other women, then we have told Kitty that she will take your place.'

Deirdre bobbed her head in a frightened way, and with shaking hands began to put on the lacemaker's pinafore. She knew that she would have to be not only as good as the other women, but better, by the end of the week. Matron was not a woman who liked being contradicted, and it was clear that she would be only too happy to see Deirdre fail.

However, as soon as Deirdre took the needle in her hand she calmed down. All through the day before, she had thought and thought about how the lace was made, and in her mind she knew exactly what to do. She listened attentively to what Miss O'Connell told them; then, taking a long piece of white cotton, she threaded the finest needle she could find.

'First of all, you must baste the cambric to the net,' began Miss O'Connell.

'What does she mean, "baste"?' whispered one of the other women.

'It means what we call tacking,' whispered back Deirdre. 'Just some temporary stitches to hold the cambric in place on the net.'

'And then,' continued Miss O'Connell, 'you'll be able to see the pattern, which I've already drawn on the net for you. You must use your best stitching to go over that pattern. It doesn't matter about the basting stitches, but the stitches over the pattern lines must be perfect. You'll spoil the cloth if you have to do much unpicking, so your work must always be right the first time.'

Deirdre did what she was told. Her head was bent over her work and her whole attention was on it. Perfection came easily to Deirdre; she was a perfectionist by nature.

From across the room, Fiona eyed her with affection. Deirdre will really enjoy this lacemaking, she thought. Fiona did not envy her; she knew that she herself was incapable of doing that fine neat work. In fact, she thought with a sigh, I can't do much with my hands at all. Even when she tried her hardest, her efforts always looked as if a child of five had done the work; even the spinning – she had never been able to manage it, and it looked as if Old Sally was not going to be any better at teaching Fiona McMahon to spin than Deirdre and Nora had been.

After half an hour of patiently putting right all the mistakes, Old Sally began to tire of Fiona. She cast an envious look across the room at Deirdre, diligently working for Miss O'Connell, and wished fervently that she could exchange the twins. However, she was a kind old woman with grandchildren of her own, and she did not want to get Fiona into trouble.

'Look, love,' she said, 'I think you're a bit tired today. I'll do the spinning, and you go and tidy the wool cupboard for me. When they brought in the sheared wool a few weeks ago, they just dumped it in the cupboard. You sort it all out. Black wool on the bottom shelf, white wool on the next shelf, and the spun wool above that. Don't put anything on the top shelf; we'll keep that for any wool we dye. It's too high for you to reach, anyway. But be sure you listen out for Matron coming, lovey, and get straight back to the spinning wheel before she opens the door. You'll hear her shoes on the flagstones.'

Fiona gladly did as she was told. There was a faint warmth in the wool cupboard, coming from some hot water pipes which ran along the back of it to stop the wool turning mouldy. Fiona found that if she half-closed the door the warmth stayed in, and soon she began to feel quite cosy. She was dreamily sorting the wool, her mind on her story – she had just decided to have roast pork for breakfast every day – when she heard her sister's name.

'That Deirdre,' Kitty was saying in a sibilant whisper, 'she's cheated me of a place in the lacemaking class. If I could learn to make lace, I'd get out of here quick. You can sell lace in Ennis for a pound a piece these days.'

There was a murmur from one of the other women, which Fiona could not understand; then Kitty's voice came again. Although she spoke in a whisper, there was a hiss in her voice which carried the words quite plainly to Fiona, who was standing silently inside the wool cupboard.

'I'm going to make sure that she won't carry on. Do you see these scissors? When we're going out, you go on one side of her and I'll go on the other, and I'll dig the points into her hand. She won't do any sewing for a week or two, I can tell you that.'

Fiona stood there with her hand on the soft wool, her face growing cold with fear. What was she to do?

At that moment she heard the clicking of Matron's shoes coming down the corridor, so she slipped silently out of her hiding-place and quickly sat down at the spinning wheel.

For the rest of the day Fiona puzzled over what to do. She couldn't warn her sister: Deirdre was sitting right beside Miss O'Connell, so there was no possibility of speaking to her. Fiona wondered whether it would do any good to talk to Old Sally, but she doubted it. Kitty was a bully and all the other women were a bit afraid of her. No, it was up to Fiona herself, and she would have to be quick and clever.

An idea came to her. At five o'clock, when all the women started to put their work away, Fiona slipped across the room, leaving the good-natured Sally to tidy away the wool which had been spun. She stood beside Deirdre and quickly started to talk to Miss O'Connell.

Fiona might not have been much good with her hands, but as her mother had often said, she could talk the hind leg off a donkey. She asked Miss O'Connell intelligent questions about lacemaking, and kept an animated conversation going, as one by one all the women left the room. Even Kitty had no further excuse for lingering.

'Would you like to learn lacemaking, too?' asked Miss O'Connell, finding the pretty brown-eyed girl so interested in the different types of lace: Limerick lace, Carrickmacross lace, *appliqué* lace, guipure lace . . .

'Oh, no,' laughed Fiona. 'I've just got it in my head that one day I'm going to be very rich, so I want to start planning my wardrobe in time!'

Miss O'Connell smiled and, gathering up her basket of sewing things, prepared to leave.

'We'll walk to the door with you,' said Fiona. 'Oh — excuse me while I just open this window. I promised Old Sally.'

Deirdre looked at her sister, puzzled. What on earth was Fiona up to?

Fiona unlatched the heavy sash window and pulled it up a little. Then she seized Deirdre by the right hand

and, carefully keeping her sister between herself and Miss O'Connell, she went out the door.

As she had guessed, Kitty was waiting, accompanied by a couple of her friends. Fiona took an even tighter hold of Deirdre's hand as they walked down the long stone corridor, keeping Miss O'Connell's attention by discussing Limerick lace. She kept talking until they reached the heavy front door. Fiona politely opened it; as soon as Miss O'Connell had gone down the path, she dragged Deirdre through and softly closed the door behind them as quickly as she could.

'Fiona, what on earth are you doing?' said Deirdre in a panic.

'Hush,' said Fiona, in a low voice. 'Trust me. Kitty's planning to attack you with her scissors and make your hand so sore that you won't be able to sew for a week. Let's climb in here.'

Bewildered but obedient, Deirdre followed Fiona through the open window down, inch by inch, and noiselessly latched it. Without saying a word, she beckoned to Deirdre to follow her; she opened the door of the wool cupboard and climbed up the shelves until she was safely on the very top shelf. Deirdre followed. They crouched there in silence, listening to the thumping of their hearts.

After about five minutes the door opened and Kitty's high-pitched voice sounded in the empty room.

'Deirdre, Fiona, where are you? Matron's looking for you.'

There was a pause. Deirdre made a slight movement, but Fiona placed a finger on her sister's lips and Deirdre froze again.

Kitty's friend Mary said, 'I told you they didn't come back in after they went to the door with Miss O'Connell. They must be still out in the yard somewhere.'

To the great relief of both girls, the door shut behind the women. The twins stretched their cramped muscles.

'Is it safe to go out now?' asked Deirdre.

'No,' said Fiona. 'We'd better stay here until we hear the bell for supper. After supper we can go straight up to the girls' dormitory and stay there until bedtime. Kitty won't dare go there – the women aren't allowed in the girls' dormitory – so we'll be safe. I think we should do the same thing tomorrow, and perhaps even the next day.'

'Oh, no,' said Deirdre, distressed. 'We can't do that. We've promised to meet Martin every evening at this time. He'll be getting worried about us.'

'Well, we can't have you getting hurt and missing your chance to learn lacemaking,' said Fiona decisively. 'Martin wouldn't want that to happen.'

I'm the practical one now, she thought in amazement. I'm the one who's making the plans. I saved Deirdre.

Fiona was so pleased with herself that – although normally she found it almost impossible to stay still for longer than a few minutes, unless she had a book to read – she crouched in the warm darkness for nearly an hour, without moving or making a single complaint.

Chapter Seven

ll that week, when work finished at five o'clock, Deirdre and Fiona hid on the top shelf of the wool cupboard. Towards the end of the week, Kitty seemed to give up hope of attacking Deirdre; but Fiona did not want to take any chances. So it was Sunday before they had a chance to see Martin and Daniel again.

All through the morning services, Deirdre and Fiona kept sending sidelong glances across the church. They could see Martin easily – he was one of the biggest boys there, so he stood out from the others – but there was no sign of Daniel anywhere in the church. Deirdre and Fiona were at the back, so they were able to look up and down the rows of boys, and by the middle of the service they were both quite certain of the truth: Daniel was not there. Deirdre kept hoping that for some reason or other he was going to the second service, but a cold feeling of dread settled in Fiona's stomach. She remembered her worries of last week. Was Daniel sick?

When the service had finished, everyone stood up and the boys filed out. Deirdre and Fiona checked a last hopeless time. No, Daniel was definitely not there – and not only that: Martin looked really sick. His face was white, with a terrible yellow tinge.

'I hope he can wait,' whispered Fiona. 'We must find out what's happened.'

Deirdre nodded. The boys had all gone out, so the girls turned to follow them. Deirdre and Fiona delayed, letting the younger girls pass by them, and then stopped in the same place. Again Fiona bent down as if to button her shoe.

'Deirdre,' said a hoarse voice.

'Oh, Martin, where's Daniel? Is he sick?'

There was a silence, and then a muffled sound. Martin was crying. Fiona bent her head even further down, feeling sick and dizzy, and Deirdre clung to the hedge for support.

'Oh, Martin,' she said. 'He's not . . . dead?'

There was a violent gulping sound, and Martin said hastily, 'No, Deirdre, he's not dead, but he – he has yellow fever. He's in the infirmary. I tried to see him, but they wouldn't let me in.'

Then Martin ran away; the girls could hear his boots thudding on the soft grass. They stood and looked at each other blankly.

'We must see him,' said Deirdre decisively. 'He's alone there in the infirmary, and he must be very frightened. He's never been away from the family before. Let's go and see Matron.'

The two girls walked down the gravelled path, going more and more slowly as they drew near Matron's office.

'Come in,' said Matron, in response to the timid knock. The girls entered the room.

Matron looked up from her desk. Two white faces – one with brown eyes and blond stubbly hair just beginning to grow back, the other with blue eyes and small tight brown curls – looked back at her. I've never seen twins so unlike each other, thought Matron. They aren't even the same size; Fiona is a good four inches taller than Deirdre. Her face hardened; perhaps they weren't twins, perhaps they were just making a fool of her. She spoke even more abruptly than usual. 'What's the matter? Hurry up, I'm busy.'

Fiona gulped and looked imploringly at Deirdre.

'It's about our brother Daniel, Ma'am,' said Deirdre. 'He's in the infirmary – he's very sick with the yellow fever. We'd like to see him, please.'

Matron looked at her sourly. 'And how do you know he is in the infirmary, pray?' she asked with heavy sarcasm.

Deirdre was silent. She could not think of anything to say. Fiona jumped in quickly, her vivid imagination immediately supplying her with a story.

'We were passing along the corridor this morning, Matron,' she said. 'And we heard some of the women from the infirmary talking. They were talking about a boy being sick with the yellow fever, a little boy with dark curly hair; and then they mentioned his name, so we knew it was our brother.'

Matron looked hard at Fiona, and Fiona stared innocently back. Like all good storytellers, she almost believed her own tale. She looked steadily at Matron; her eyes did not water, and no blush came to her cheeks.

Matron guessed that the girls had probably heard the story from their elder brother. Despite the fact that families in different sections of the workhouse were supposed to have nothing to do with each other, it was very hard to enforce that rule. Still, she could not prove it, and there was a possibility that Fiona's story was true.

'Speak when you're spoke to,' she snapped, and turned back to Deirdre. 'It is completely impossible for you to go the infirmary,' she said. 'No one is allowed in the infirmary unless they're working there. Your brother will probably die anyway. In fact, he's probably dead already. I haven't had the death list yet this morning.

She rose to her feet and twitched her long woollen cloak from its peg behind the door; then, pushing the two girls out in front of her, she locked her office door with one of the keys from the big bunch which, like a jailer, she carried everywhere with her.

Deirdre and Fiona watched her in despair as she strutted down the corridor on her way to the second service of the day.

'I hope that God never forgives her, and that she goes to hell when she dies,' said Fiona, with her teeth clenched and her voice hard and bitter.

Deirdre said nothing. There's no point in saying anything, she thought drearily. It might make Fiona feel better to say things like that, but it never worked for Deirdre. She wished she could work on her lace. That might help to take away the horrible pain that was swelling inside her throat and chest. She didn't want to think about Daniel.

The twins went slowly to the dormitory and sat down on their bed. Deirdre forced her mind to dwell on the different stitches which she was using on the lace handkerchief. Without vanity, she knew that her needlework was as good as possible – in fact, Miss O'Connell had said she was the best neddlewoman she had ever met – but Deirdre thought she would have liked a better pattern. She wondered whether Miss O'Connell would allow her to design a pattern.

She shut her eyes, in order to concentrate better and to avoid looking at Fiona's tear-streaked face, as she tried to imagine a pattern of her own. I'd use three different kinds of flowers, she thought, and I'd have ivy twining in and out of them . . .

She opened her eyes – and then widened them. Fiona was gone.

Deirdre jumped off the bed, went to the door and looked out. There was no sign of Fiona anywhere. I'll have to go and look for her, she thought, a bit alarmed. What's she up to?

Then she stopped. They had been ordered to stay in the dormitories for the afternoon. If Deirdre went out, she would be breaking a rule, and Matron would punish her by giving her lacemaking place to Kitty; and the lacemaking was their only chance of getting out of the workhouse. With a heavy heart, Deirdre turned around and went back to sit on the bed.

Meanwhile, Fiona was crossing the yard towards the infirmary.

She had not been able to bear sitting there for another minute. It's no good, she thought. I'm not like Deirdre,

I can't just accept things. Softly she stole out of the room, her shoes in her hand. I know it's stupid, she told herself, as she went down the stone stairs. I know what Deirdre would say, and I suppose she's right, but I must see Daniel. He'll be so frightened . . .

She looked nervously around the hall, but there was no sign of anyone. Softly she opened the door and crossed the yard, keeping well out of sight of the high windows, so that Matron would not be able to see her if she looked out.

When she drew near the infirmary she stopped, appalled. Even from a distance of fifty yards she could hear the groans and the cries. A woman came out of the door carrying a basket of foul, stinking linen. Fiona shrank back and winced as the smell hit her, but once the woman had disappeared into the washhouse, she went on steadily. Standing on her toes, she peeped in at the infirmary window.

Never could she have imagined such a terrible scene. Men and boys lay huddled on the floor, some with only straw to lie on. Many of them were writhing and groaning in pain. There was filth everywhere, and the smell of sickness filled the air. Fiona was white with shock.

And then she saw him. Daniel was lying on a heap of straw, next to some other boys. They were all very yellow-looking, and they all seemed to be asleep. At least he doesn't look as if he's in pain, Fiona thought, wiping away the tears that poured down her cheeks. I wonder whether I could manage to steal in and see him – or would it be bad to wake him up?

Suddenly a hard hand seized her and she was jerked back, away from the window, around the corner of the building. For a moment Fiona thought it was Matron; then she realised that it was only Martin.

'What are you doing?' he hissed.

Fiona pushed him away angrily. He had given her a dreadful fright. 'I'm just trying to see Daniel,' she said. 'Anyway, what are you doing? I don't suppose you're allowed here, either.'

'I followed you,' said Martin briefly. 'You can't do Daniel any good. You'll only get yourself into trouble. Get back, as quickly as you can.'

Without a word, he turned on his heel and left her.

Deirdre was wide-eyed and tense with anxiety by the time Fiona came back.

'Where have you been?' she whispered.

'I tried to see Daniel,' said Fiona, struggling to get the words out through her sobs. 'Oh, Deirdre, he's in the infirmary, and it's terrible. I could never have imagined anything so bad.'

Deirdre's eyes widened even more, but she did not stir as Fiona tried to find words for the horrors she had seen. Fiona could see her sister's hands clench together.

'What will we do, Deirdre?' she whispered, looking despairingly at her twin.

Deirdre opened her hands and took a deep breath. 'Do you remember what Ma used to say, Fiona? "What can't be cured must be endured." We can't help Daniel now. What can we do for him? You were right not to go in to him; sleep is the best thing for him. We must all just endure until we can find some way out.'

Even Fiona was glad to enter the sewing room on Monday morning. In the last couple of days she had started to tell Old Sally the story of *Oliver Twist*, which Fiona had read and reread so often that she almost knew it by heart. Old Sally was so thrilled, and so interested in the story, that she was willing to go on covering up for the fact that Fiona was learning very little and actually doing almost nothing.

When five o'clock came, Deirdre determinedly got to her feet. They must see Martin that evening and find out whether there was any news about Daniel. She doubted that Kitty would make any attempt to hurt her now; it was obvious to everyone that Miss O'Connell found Deirdre the best of her students, and she would never be willing to have her replaced by Kitty for any reason.

Quickly Deirdre grabbed Fiona by the hand, and they were first out of the sewing room. They went along the girls' yard and across the path, to the hedge at the side of the boys' yard. Fiona, without being told, bent down to button her shoe, and Deirdre whispered, 'Martin.'

There was no answer. She tried again, slightly louder this time, but still there was no answer. They could hear the other boys still talking and playing – so where was Martin?

Fiona got to her feet and looked at her sister in a worried way. 'Perhaps he thought we weren't coming because we didn't last week,' she whispered. 'Try again.'

Deirdre tried again, a little louder; and then again, louder still. Still no answer. They heard the bell signalling the end of the boys' recreation time, and then the heavy boots clumping in.

In desperation, Deirdre raised her voice to its normal pitch. 'Martin!' she said.

From the other side of the hedge a gruff voice said, 'Who's there? Is that Martin's sister?'

'Yes,' said Deirdre, dropping her voice back down to a whisper. 'Is he there?'

There was a short pause, and then the strange boy spoke again, pity and embarrassment making his voice even more gruff.

'Martin has the yellow fever. He's in the infirmary. I must go. 'Bye.'

Deirdre and Fiona stood there as if turned into stone. They felt that they could hardly bear this new sorrow. First Daniel and now Martin . . .

They never knew how they managed to get through supper. Time after time Fiona took up her spoon and then set it down again. Even Deirdre, who was normally determined to eat every scrap of food she could get, no matter how disgusting, could not manage to swallow more than a mouthful.

When bedtime came they lay silently side by side, staring at the ceiling. From time to time a sob shook Fiona's body, but Deirdre was tearless.

When they heard the clock over the gate strike midnight, Deirdre made a great effort.

'Fiona,' she said softly. 'Fiona, I've been thinking. We mustn't give up hope. Yellow fever isn't nearly as bad as the black fever that Ma and Da died of. Martin and Daniel are both very healthy. They're never sick, and they've both been working out of doors for the whole winter; and they've had enough food, not like most of the people who die of the fever. I think they have a good chance. But I know one thing, Fiona: we must get out of this workhouse. There are too many sick people here. When Martin and Daniel get better we must try to leave, as soon as we can.'

Fiona took a deep breath. There was a calm certainty about Deirdre which made her feel better. She began to feel sleepy. Soon she was asleep; but Deirdre stayed awake for another hour, thinking and planning.

Chapter Eight

The next three weeks seemed endless. Deirdre worked as hard as she could at her lacemaking, putting every ounce of her skill and her intelligence into creating an article of beauty. Miss O'Connell gave Fiona an empty copybook and a pencil, so she spent all her spare time writing stories to read to the younger children in the dormitory. Old Sally still loved *Oliver Twist*, but some of the younger children found the story a bit upsetting; so Fiona set to work to write happy, funny stories which would keep them amused. She also had a piece of broken slate and a slate-pencil, and with those she went over and over the mathematics she had learned in school. She was determined to forget nothing. And every night, before she went to sleep, she repeated to herself one of the poems from the Sixth Reader. If nothing else, at least it stopped her thinking about Martin and Daniel.

It was on the first day of June that hope began to come back to the twins. It was a Sunday, and they were in their usual seat at the back of the church, when something familiar halfway up the church caught Fiona's eye. It was a head of brown curls – rather longer than they had been the last time she had seen them, but Fiona was certain.

'Deirdre,' she said in a whisper. 'Is that Daniel?'

Deirdre looked, and her heart began to pound. She felt a glow of joy right through her. It was certainly Daniel.

She looked back at the older boys, but there was still no sign of Martin. Never mind, she thought; he got the yellow fever a week after Daniel, so it will take him another week to recover. He'll certainly recover if Daniel did. Martin is the strongest person I've ever known.

Deirdre was right. By the next Sunday, Martin, looking rather tired and shaky, was back in his place in church. From then on, none of them missed the daily exchange of news through the hedge. Martin usually had more to say than the girls, because the man who was teaching him gardening, Mr Duggan, came from near

Kilfenora, so he was able to give Martin news of all that was happening around Drumshee.

It was he who told Martin that the schoolmaster had gone to America. The news upset Fiona at first but then Deirdre pointed out that if there was no real teacher at Inchovea School, the neighbours might be willing to pay Fiona something to teach the little children. Fiona tossed her head and said, 'I'll be able to teach any of them, small or big'; but secretly she was delighted at the idea and worked even harder at her lessons.

Martin was more interested in another of Mr Duggan's pieces of news: the surprising information that their landlord, Mr O'Brien, had been unable to rent out any of his fourteen farms – including Drumshee – and that he owed so much money on unpaid taxes that he had abandoned all the farms and gone to America himself.

Miss O'Connell was also able to give them some information about the world outside the workhouse. She had taken a great fancy to Deirdre, and when she heard about the terrible Sundays she managed to get permission from Matron for Deirdre, accompanied by Fiona, to come and have tea at her tiny house at Lahinch, near the sea. Matron was very reluctant to allow the girls this pleasure, but the Board of Guardians was so astonished and pleased at the amount of money that the lacemaking was earning for the workhouse that Matron was afraid to refuse Miss O'Connell anything.

And so on Sunday afternoons, Deirdre and Miss O'Connell worked together on drawing the patterns for the week's lacemaking, and Deirdre helped Miss O'Connell with her private lacemaking work, while Fiona buried herself in one of Miss O'Connell's books.

'You must let me give you some money for this, Deirdre,' remarked Miss O'Connell, one cold November afternoon when the three of them were sitting cosily in front of the fire. 'I sold that lace skirt in Ennis last week for eight pounds, and you must have stitched nearly a quarter of it.'

Deirdre's eyes shone with excitement at the mention of such a sum of money, and even Fiona lifted her head. Miss O'Connell noticed the eager look in Deirdre's eyes and took a pound note out of her purse. 'Will this be enough?' she said.

Deirdre shook her head vigorously. 'Oh, no, I couldn't take any money from you. I'm happy to be able to help you. I was only pleased at the idea of being able to make so much money. We're all hoping to leave the workhouse one day, and we'll need money to buy food.'

'Well, won't you take this and save it? I'll pay you for as much work as you can do for me.'

Deirdre shook her head again. 'I don't want to take money from you, Miss O'Connell. You've been so kind to me. In any case, I have nowhere to keep it; Matron would be bound to find it and take it away from me.'

Miss O'Connell thought for a few minutes and then said decisively, 'I'll tell you what we'll do. I'll keep a box here, and when you do any work for me I'll put your share of the money in the box. Whenever you want it, you'll only have to ask me for it. And, Deirdre, I have more orders for lace than I can possibly get made. These days, every fine lady wants lace in her clothing. They say that Queen Victoria herself has ordered a dress with an overskirt of Limerick lace, and a bonnet trimmed to match. I was wondering about giving up my work at the workhouse, but I don't want to – it's a steady wage, and I want to save up as much money as possible, because I'm going to London at the end of April. I wonder whether Matron would allow you and Fiona to come around here every evening at five o'clock? We could work together, and then I could bring you back to the workhouse at bedtime. What do you think? Would you find it too much work for you?'

'Oh, Miss O'Connell,' said Deirdre, her eyes shining with delight, 'I'd like nothing better. I've often wished I could work at my lace in the evenings, instead of sitting in that cold dormitory, but I've always been afraid to ask.'

'Well, that's settled, then,' said Miss O'Connell. 'And I know Fiona will want to come too when she hears that I'm getting a copy of Mr Charles Dickens's new book, *A Christmas Carol*. She can sit and read to us while we work.'

The winter of 1846 to 1847 was the worst that anyone alive could remember. Snow fell thick and heavy, and the rivers were frozen for weeks on end. All around the villages of Lahinch, Ennistymon and Kilfenora the people died of famine and disease; and within the workhouse, the inmates shivered with cold and slowly starved from the lack of good nourishing food. Everywhere there was disease – black fever, yellow fever, dysentery and scurvy. The infirmary at the back of the workhouse was full, and the sheds which were hastily built behind the vegetable gardens were rapidly filling up as well.

Of all the inmates in the workhouse, Deirdre and Fiona were the best off. Miss O'Connell always gave them a good meal in the evening; her brother was a well-off farmer, and he kept her well supplied with sausages and bacon and home-baked bread, and also with plenty of turf. The little one-roomed house was as warm as toast.

Both girls looked forward to evenings and Sundays with great eagerness. Fiona sat by the blazing fire, her feet cosily warm, and read from *A Christmas Carol,* and Miss O'Connell and Deirdre sat at the table sewing busily. Miss O'Connell's brother had bought her a lacemaker's lamp. It was like an ordinary oil lamp, but it had a globe filled with water beside it; the globe magnified the flame from the lamp, casting a good strong light on the work.

They were making another overskirt, and this time Deirdre had helped to design it. She had always been very good at drawing, and she had persuaded Miss O'Connell that they might get a better price for a completely new design that was not in any of the pattern books. Fiona thought the skirt was going to be beautiful. The net base was covered with butterflies of all different sizes, with the antennae sewn with the tiniest of stitches and the fringed wings carefully outlined. Fiona was not surprised when the overskirt was sold to someone called Lady Rosalind Fitzgerald, in Corofin, for nine pounds.

By the middle of February, the two girls were spending most of their free time in Miss O'Connell's little house. They even slept there; Miss O'Connell had told Matron that the weather was too cold and the snow too deep for the girls to walk back in the evenings, so they slept cosily on a feather mattress in front of the fire. The only problem was that they could only talk to Martin and Daniel once a week, after church on Sundays. However, the boys understood. Martin could hardly believe it when Deirdre told him that the money in the box on the mantelpiece added up to eight pounds.

At the end of March, the weather began to improve. There was a softness in the wind; the snow and ice melted away, and the wet fields began to show a flush of green through their winter brown. The infirmary, however, was as full as ever, and in the streets of Kilfenora and Ennistymon the starving people still died of hunger and disease.

Fiona was worried about Old Sally. The old woman was coughing continuously, and Fiona had to do her best to help her with the spinning – the poor old woman hardly had the strength to turn the wheel. Fiona was still bad at spinning. No matter how much she tried – and she really did try – she still found it terribly difficult. As often as she could, Deirdre left her own work and came to help Fiona; but even so, Fiona lived in fear that Matron would notice how little wool was being spun these days.

One Saturday halfway through April, Fiona's worst fears were realised. She came into the sewing room in the morning to find no one sitting at the spinning wheel. While she was standing there, looking around in bewilderment, Matron came across to her.

'Old Sally died last night,' she said harshly. 'Not that she'll be much loss. She was getting too old to be useful. You must be able to manage on your own, girl. Well, go on – there's no time to waste.'

Fiona's eyes filled with tears, but she was given no time to mourn Old Sally. She hastily seated herself at the spinning wheel and fumbled with the thread. She could almost feel Matron's sharp grey eyes boring into her.

The thread broke. Fiona tried to twist it together. It broke again. She looked across the room at Deirdre, but it was no good. There was nothing Deirdre could do for her now.

The silence in the sewing room was so intense that you could almost feel it. Everyone knew that Matron was working herself into one of her rages. Every head was bent over the work; even the snip of scissors and the click of knitting-needles sounded muted in that silent room.

Fiona was in agony. Again and again the thread broke.

Finally she gave up in despair and just sat there, her head bowed and her hands resting in her lap. In a way, she thought, it's almost a relief to give up.

The next moment, Fiona's head jerked up as she received a stinging slap which rang through the whole room.

Deirdre prayed wordlessly, but it was no good. Fiona was on her feet and both her cheeks were flaming red.

'Don't you hit me, you horrible woman!'

If the silence had been intense before, it was almost deafening now. Everyone stopped work and stared at Matron, and Deirdre was not the only one who was holding her breath.

Matron was an odd colour, more purple than red, with a greyish tinge under the flush; and when her voice came it was a hoarse croak.

'Kitty, Mary, to the punishment cell with her. She can cool her heels there until Sunday night. And on Monday morning, Miss Fiona, you can go and help in the infirmary. There are plenty of floor to scrub and bedlinen to wash there. You won't waste any more time here in the sewing room, my fine lady.'

As Kitty and Mary dragged Fiona out, Miss O'Connell gently squeezed Deirdre's hand. Deirdre knew what that squeeze meant. It was showing sympathy, but it was also warning her not to get mixed up in her sister's disgrace.

Deirdre returned the squeeze timidly. She knew what she had to do, and she sewed on without hesitating.

Chapter Nine

The punishment cell was a small room with a stone floor, stone walls and a single tiny window at the top of the wall. In the corner was a heap of straw for a bed. In the half-darkness Fiona could see that the walls were running with damp, and the floor was wet under her feet.

She sat on the heap of straw and buried her face in her hands. Already she had begun to shake with cold. Two days! How could she possibly stand two days locked in here with no one to talk to?

She tried her best to keep her mind off the threat that she would be sent to work at the infirmary. Can Matron really do that? she wondered. After all, I'm only twelve years old . . . She tried to tell herself that Matron was only trying to frighten her, but deep down she knew that Matron would do whatever she wanted – and what she wanted was to get rid of Fiona.

The hours passed. Fiona watched the patch of sunlight move slowly around the walls, until there was very little light left.

From behind the wall came a scuffling sound. Fiona almost bit through her lip. If there was one thing that she dreaded, it was rats. It's only mice, she told herself, and tried to steady the thumping of her heart.

She was determined not to scream for help or knock on the door. She knew that it would do no good, and if Matron heard her it would only giver her satisfaction.

What a pity I didn't hit her back, Fiona thought. I might as well have done. There's no hope for me now. If I go to the infirmary, I'll probably be dead before summer comes.

No one came to bring Fiona a meal or a drink, and when the cell grew completely dark she gave up hope. She tried to sleep on the straw, but it was impossible. Her body was rigid was cold.

When morning came Fiona was dazed and giddy. She tried to stand up, but sank down again. There was a little ray of sunshine coming in through the high window, but it did nothing to warm the cell. She was almost sleepy; she felt as if nothing mattered much. When a key grated in the lock and the door opened, she hardly turned her head.

'Here's some porridge for you, Fiona,' said Kitty's voice.

Fiona made no answer. Mary's voice, rather alarmed, said: 'She looks really sick, Kitty. Let's try and get some porridge into her.'

Kitty put the porridge down on the straw, but Fiona was too weak and cold even to move her head. Mary – who, as Deirdre always said, was a naturally kind woman when away from Kitty's influence – knelt down in the straw and put her arm around Fiona. She held Fiona in a half-sitting position and began to spoon the hot porridge into her as if she were a baby.

After a few minutes, Fiona began to feel more awake. She started to shiver violently. Funnily enough, the shivering seemed to warm her, and by the time the bowl of porridge was finished she was feeling better.

'Come on,' said Kitty impatiently. 'There's the bell for church. We must get her out of here. She's to sit beside Matron in the church. Let's bring her in now.'

So Fiona was escorted into church by her jailers and put sitting beside Matron. She dared not lift her head or look around for Deirdre or her brothers; she sat still, praying that she would not be put back in the punishment cell.

Her prayers were not answered. When the service was over, Kitty and Mary half-dragged her back to the cell.

It was dark by the time they came to release her. She was taken back to the girls' dormitory. To her enormous relief, Deirdre had not gone to Miss O'Connell's house that night; she was there, awake and waiting.

'Oh, Deirdre,' said Fiona, in a sobbing whisper, as she slid into bed.

Deirdre made no reply; she put her finger warningly on her sister's lips, then wrapped her arms around the ice-cold body. Fiona snuggled into her, starting to feel warm for the first time in two days, and soon she had dropped off to sleep.

When she woke up, for a moment she did not know where she was; but then she felt her sister's finger on her lips again. Deirdre spoke in Fiona's ear, her words almost as noiseless as a sigh.

'Fiona,' she said. 'Get dressed without making any sound. We're going to run away.'

A feeling of excitement and hope welled up in Fiona. Deirdre had planed something; and usually Deirdre's plans were carefully worked out.

They both dressed and wrapped themselves in their shawls, which hung on pegs beside the bed. Deirdre looked carefully around the room; then, holding her shoes in her hand, she stole out. Fiona followed her. The corridor was very dark, but they knew it so well that they went along it with confidence, treading softly and keeping close to the wall.

It seemed like a lifetime before they reached the big door at the front of the workhouse. Deirdre drew back the heavy iron bolts, wincing at the scraping noise they made, and then they were outside in the open.

They put on their shoes and walked down the path, carefully keeping close to the hedge. Fiona wondered why Deirdre was leading her to the back of the work-house. They went past the infirmary, to the vegetables gardens; here Deirdre left the path and stepped across the neat rows until she reached the hedge at the far side. Fiona followed obediently and without saying a word, but when they had gone through the hedge she gave a start: two figures were standing in the shadows.

Her fright only lasted a moment, however; then she realised that the figures were her brothers. Martin grabbed her hand, Deirdre took Daniel, and the four of them set off, running as fast as they could along the narrow grassy lane which led to Ennistymon.

No one spoke. The danger was still too near. A few times Fiona thought she heard someone shout, but it was only the noise of the blood thumping in her ears.

When they reached the bridge at Ennistymon, they slipped down the side of it and walked along beside the river, completely hidden by the thick fringe of trees that grew along the bank. They still did not dare to talk, however, in case some gamekeeper might be out looking for poachers. It was only when they were safely out of Ennistymon and climbing the steep hill to the Ballagh Road that Fiona broke the silence.

'Deirdre,' she said, 'are we going back to Drumshee? Oh, I can't believe it! Are we really going home?'

'We planned it all yesterday,' said Martin eagerly. 'As soon as we knew what had happened to you, we knew we'd have to run away. We couldn't let you go to the infirmary. Even one day there might be enough to give you a fever.'

'Martin has some turnip seed in his pocket to plant at Drumshee,' piped up Daniel, wanting his share in the conversation.

'How are we going to manage, though, for food and everything else?' asked Fiona.

'Well,' said Deirdre, 'Miss O'Connell gave me the nine pounds from the savings box, and she also gave me some pieces of net and cambric, so I can go on making lace. She's going to London next week, but she says I'll easily be able to sell my lace in Ennis market, or to Lady Rosalind Fitzgerald in Corofin. So I can go on earning money. In the meantime, we can use some of the money to buy Indian meal.'

'And we might even have some oats left in the storeroom,' said Martin. 'We can use some to make porridge, and I'll sow the rest.'

They had reached Lake Lickeen, and there was still no sound of pursuit. Martin doubted that there would be much of a search for them. After all, the workhouse was full; every day hungry, desperate people were turned away from it. He was old enough to leave, and no one would really bother about Daniel.

The girls were a different matter. Matron probably would not want to lose Deirdre, because her lace made money for the workhouse. She might also, out of spite, not want to let Fiona go.

But on the whole, Martin thought, once we're safely back in Drumshee, no one from the workhouse will worry about us.

Chapter Ten

The four children were within a mile of Drumshee when the moon finally broke through the dark clouds. Now they could see the truth of what Mr Duggan had told Martin: stables and cabins were ruined and broken, there were no cows in the fields, no smoke came from the houses which were still standing, and the potato ridges were broken and scattered.

Drumshee itself was completely surrounded by trees; so even after the children had turned in at the gates and were climbing the steep hill of the avenue, they had no idea of whether the house still stood or whether the thatch had been dragged off and the stone walls tumbled, as in so many cottages they had seen. No one spoke until they came over the brow of the hill – and there, in the white moonlight, was the cottage at Drumshee.

'I can't believe it,' said Deirdre in a low voice.

'Hurray! We're home!' shouted Daniel.

'Hush,' said Martin. 'Listen.'

They all stopped and listened. There was something moving in the undergrowth by the trees, and it was coming nearer. The moonlight picked out a glare from a pair of yellow eyes.

Fiona's overwrought nerves gave way and she screamed – a short sound, bitten back as soon as she regained control over herself, but it was enough to break the stillness and tension in the air. Martin launched himself into the undergrowth. There was a struggle, branches snapped, Martin swore; and then the sound of his laugh, high and cracked, came from the bushes.

'Don't worry, Fiona,' he said. 'It's only Billy and his wives. I've managed to catch one of the nanny goats. I'll put her in one of the cabins. We can milk her in the morning.'

Deirdre, Fiona, and Daniel all started to laugh. Suddenly they became children again, and it was as if nothing so funny had ever happened to them in their lives. Tears streamed from their eyes. They stood on the avenue and laughed and laughed, holding their sides and wiping their faces, while Martin, with his hand securely twisted in the nanny goat's hair, dragged her into the cabin and wedged a big stone against the door.

'Now for the house,' he said, as he returned. They all followed him into the little stone cottage.

It seemed to them as if it had been a hundred years, instead of only just over a year, since they had left Drumshee; but everything was just as they had left it. There were the embers of the last fire they had lit, and beside the hearth was some wood, ready stacked. Martin looked pleased.

'I'd forgotten we left wood,' he said. 'That's great – we'll get a fire going. It doesn't feel too damp either. Daniel, you stack the timber in the fireplace while I get down the tinderbox.'

Martin stood on a stone stool to reach the little cupboard, set high in the wall by the fireplace, where the tinderbox was kept. The tinder was a little damp, but after a few attempts he struck a flame, and soon they had a fire burning.

It was wonderful. The room's very dusty, thought Deirdre, but we'll soon put that right. The important thing is that we're home, and home is still here.

She yawned happily, less out of tiredness than from relief after the tension of the last few days.

'I wonder what that hay is like, that we put in the storeroom,' said Martin.

'Probably pretty mouldy,' said Daniel, who was yawning as well.

'I think we should try to get our bedsteads out of the storeroom,' said Martin. 'I know it's dark, but there's a good moon, and we're all so tired that we'll be no use until we have a sleep.'

No one objected. Although they were excited, they were all beginning to feel a bit sleepy.

They climbed the steep path to the fort. The moon was very bright, and they could see their way quite clearly. Martin had a slight fear that their underground stores might have been discovered by somebody desperate with hunger, but the slab and the grass over it seemed to be undisturbed.

Even when they were underground, they could still see the moonlight shining brightly down the stone steps; they had plenty of light to drag out their bedsteads. One by one, they carried them down the hill and set them up in the kitchen, beside the fire.

Then Martin and Daniel went back for the hay. It was surprisingly good, considering it had spent a year underground, and it was dry enough for them to sleep on. Most people would have found it a bit scratchy, but the four children were so tired that they were asleep almost as soon as they lay down.

They slept until well after sunrise. It was Fiona who woke everyone up. She had been having a nightmare; she sat up, breathless and tearful, and could not believe what she was seeing. There she was, back home, warm and snug; her brother and Deirdre were beside her, the fire was still burning, and bright spring sunshine was pouring in through the window.

'Wake up, everyone!' she said happily. 'We're home!'

The others yawned and stretched and tumbled out of bed. Martin fetched a few pots from the storeroom and milked the nanny goat; Daniel got the fire going, while Deirdre swept the kitchen floor and took from her bag a cake of soda bread and some butter which Miss O'Connell had given her. Fiona filled the big iron pot with water from the well and hung it on the iron crane over the fireplace: when they had finished their breakfast, there would be hot water to help them get everything clean again.

Daniel disappeared after he had got the fire going; he came back with an armful of twigs and a grin that stretched from ear to ear.

'Guess what I found in the hedge,' he said, setting down the wood and putting his hand in his pocket. One by one, very carefully, he took out four eggs.

'Oh, it must be Higglety!' said Fiona happily. 'She must be still here.'

'It might be one of her chicks,' said Daniel. 'You remember how Martin said they'd go to make dinners for the landlord? Well, I don't think he bothered. I think all our animals, except the horse and the pig and the cows, are probably still around.'

When Martin came back with the goat's milk, he was astonished by the sound of eggs bubbling in the frying pan. Deirdre had sacrificed a lump of Miss O'Connell's precious butter to fry them in, and nothing ever tasted as delicious as that breakfast of eggs, warm milk and soda bread.

Martin agreed with Daniel. He had seen at least three more goats hanging around near the cabin where he had put the first one, and Billy himself was certainly there.

'After breakfast I'm going to get some oats and see if I can get the ducks back,' said Fiona. 'I wonder whether Spooky is still around.'

Spooky, the black and white duck, had been a great pet of Fiona's. Fiona called her Spooky because she had been so nervous and jumpy when she was a duckling. It had taken Fiona a lot of time and patience to tame her; but in the end she had become very friendly, landing on Fiona's shoulder and nuzzling into her neck. If any duck was going to come back, Spooky would definitely be the one.

'Don't take too much of the oats,' said Martin. 'I'm hoping they're still good enough for us to eat for a few days. I know Deirdre has enough money to pay for Indian meal, but I'd prefer to keep away from towns and shops for a few days, until we're sure nobody's looking for us.'

They finished their breakfast and, chattering happily, went up to the storeroom in the fort. They were surprised at how well things had lasted. The hay-bags, which Deirdre had hung on a stick, were damp, but they had no holes in them; the oats in their sealed pots smelt quite fresh; and even Fiona's cherished *Oliver Twist* came out of its wax-sealed box looking almost as fresh as the day it had been put there. Fiona eyed it longingly, but with a great effort of will she put it aside. There was too much to do, and she knew that she would have to do most of the rough housework and look after the ducks and the hens. It was important to keep Deirdre's hands smooth and soft. The family depended on Deirdre's lacemaking to earn money for food.

One by one, all the things were taken out of the storeroom. The pots were scrubbed, the hay-bags were washed and put out in the sunshine to dry, the beds were set up in the bedrooms, the table was put by the window and the spinning wheel by the fire. When everything was neat and tidy, Deirdre sat at the table to do some lacemaking, Daniel went out to search the hedgerows for eggs, Martin put on his father's bee-keeping hat and veil and went to rob the bees of a year's supply of honey, and Fiona took a handful of oats and went out to the duck pond.

She stood on the top of the bank, her blond hair – which had grown quite long again – streaming over her shoulders, her face turned up to the sun. Once again, she could hardly believe in such happiness.

Until that moment, Fiona had carefully avoided thinking about her father and mother; but suddenly she found she could think of them without pain. She imagined them in heaven, up in the blue sky she could see over Oaghty, looking down on their children and blessing them. I know everything is going to go well, she thought.

Even as she thought it, there was a rapid beating of wings, and a handsome black and white duck landed on her shoulder. Spooky had come home. A minute later the other ducks arrived, and then the drake.

'Oh, good!' said Daniel, coming up behind Fiona. 'Plenty of nice duck eggs. Oh, look, Fiona – there goes

Martin, with a thousand bees after him. Look at the amount of honey he's carrying! And guess what? Higglety is sitting on a clutch of eggs just inside that clump of blackthorn down by the river, near the waterfall. We'll soon have chicks.'

Chapter Eleven

It was nearly the middle of June before Deirdre had made enough lace to have a selection to sell. By then, nearly all the money she had brought from the workhouse had been used up on buying Indian meal and oats. Martin had spent two pounds on some special seed potatoes which had been grown high on the mountains of Donegal, where there had been no disease, and he was hoping for a crop this year.

They were all praying that no new landlord would appear to take over the farm; they had no money left for the rent.

However, they were healthy and happy and well-fed. All the goats were giving milk, and Fiona managed to make some cheese and some rather odd-tasting butter. To their surprise, some of the cabbage had seeded itself, so they had fresh greens every day. And Daniel had developed a deadly aim with his catapult; hardly a day went by without him bringing in a pigeon or a rabbit for the pot. They made rough bread from Indian meal or ground oats, and they had porridge and milk and honey every morning for breakfast.

But Martin could not stop worrying about the fact that they had no money for the rent. He remembered how carefully his father would put the money away every year. He used to hide it in a special lead box with a strange interlacing pattern engraved on it, Martin remembered, and the box was always kept in a little hollow behind a loose stone in the cupboard above the fireplace.

'How much do you think you'll get for your lace?' he asked Deirdre in a worried way.

'I'm not sure,' said Deirdre. 'I was thinking I might not go to Ennis market with it after all. Miss O'Connell told me she got a very good price for her lace from Lady Rosalind Fitzgerald in Corofin; now that Miss O'Connell has gone to London, I might be able to sell some of my lace to Lady Rosalind. I think I'll walk there tomorrow. It's so much nearer than Ennis that it's worth a try.'

'Let me come with you,' begged Fiona. 'I'd love to see Lady Rosalind, and her big house, and all her books – she even has a special room for them, called a library. Do you remember Miss O'Connell telling us about it?'

'Oh, yes, do come,' said Deirdre, brightening up at the idea. 'I was dreading going there, but now you can do the talking for me.'

'I don't think there will be much need for talking,' said Fiona thoughtfully, looking at the beautiful piece of lace spread out on the table. It was triangular, and it was meant to be worn around the shoulders. Deirdre had not used any pattern from a lacemaking book; she had drawn the shapes herself, from the different ferns which grew around the cottage. There was the solid shape of the hart's-tongue fern, the fringed lances of the bladder fern, and the tiny round shapes, dangling from their delicate stems, of the maidenhair fern.

'As soon as she sees this, she'll want it,' Fiona said, taking up the exquisite piece and looking at it admiringly.

Martin had set up a table for Deirdre outside the front door, so that she could have fresh air and plenty of light while she worked. There had always been four large square stones lying there; the McMahons had often sat on them on fine summer evenings, but it was only when Martin brought out an old door and placed it on top of the stones that the children realised that the boulders could act as the legs of a table.

'I bet someone else had a table there, once,' said Fiona.

'It might have been for a feast where they didn't have enough room inside the house,' said Daniel, happily imagining the special occasion.

'So how much do you think Lady Rosalind will pay for your lace, Deirdre?' Martin asked again.

'I'm not sure,' said Deirdre hesitantly. 'Perhaps five pounds.'

'Five pounds!' Daniel was overawed. 'Oh, Martin, we could buy a pony – the cart is still there . . .'

'Oh, no,' said Martin quickly. 'We must keep the money for rent, in case a new landlord turns up.'

But even as he spoke, the vision of a strong Connemara pony came into his mind and he felt terribly tempted. There was no denying the fact that Martin was having to do a man's work – in fact, two men's work – when he was only a growing boy of fourteen. A pony would be wonderful. He could use it to haul turf from the bog for their winter fires; it could pull a hay rake, or the light plough which they had stored so carefully in the storeroom . . . The back-breaking, cruel toil would be cut in half by a good pony.

The other three watched the struggle in his face.

'A pony would be useful for me, too, you know, Martin,' said Deirdre. 'Ennis is too far away for me to walk to very often, and I do need to get there, to sell my work and to buy net and cambric and silks.

'In any case,' she added, as she saw him still struggling with the temptation, 'you know I'll be able to earn more money after this. I'm getting quicker all the time.'

Martin's face lit up. 'You're quite right,' he said. 'In any case, even if there is a new landlord, he probably won't ask for the rent before Michaelmas – and that's at the end of September, three months away. Let's get a pony, then, if you get a good price from Lady Rosalind. We'll give ourselves a holiday on Saturday, and we'll all go into Ennis. You and Fiona can go to Corofin tomorrow; then you'll have two days to rest before the walk to Ennis.'

So the next morning, Deirdre and Fiona got up early. They washed themselves very carefully, rinsing their hair in pure rainwater scented with lavender flowers from the garden, just as their mother always had, and combing it over their shoulders to dry on the walk.

The sun was already warm when they set out, but neither of them minded. They had both worked so hard during the past few months – Deirdre with her lacemaking and Fiona with cooking and cleaning and gardening – that it seemed wonderful to have nothing to do but walk along the dusty silent road.

Deirdre had her precious lace in her basket, and Fiona had some buttermilk and some soda bread in hers. Just before they came into the village of Corofin, they stopped at the side of the road and had their meal. It was only then that Deirdre noticed that there was something else, carefully wrapped in brown paper, in the bottom of Fiona's basket.

Fiona flushed when she saw her looking. 'I suppose it's a stupid idea,' she said, 'but I was wondering about asking Lady Rosalind about my stories. Miss O'Connell said she was very nice and very friendly. After all, you told me that she was the one who arranged for Miss O'Connell to go to London and demonstrate Irish lacemaking there. I thought that if she seemed interested, I might ask her if she would read some of my stories and tell me if they're any good. I won't say anything until after you're fixed up about the lace. I mightn't say anything at all. I'll decide when I get there.'

'I think your stories are wonderful,' said Deirdre warmly. 'They're so exciting – I don't know where you get all the ideas from. And it's great the way you do some writing every night, no matter how tired you are. I think you should ask Lady Rosalind. But even if she doesn't like them, you mustn't give up. Do you remember how everyone in the workhouse used to like listening to you? You might end up as famous as Mr Charles Dickens.'

Fiona laughed happily and swallowed the last of the soda bread. They both got up and shook the crumbs from their dresses. Suddenly feeling rather nervous, they walked through Corofin and in the tall iron gates of the big house near the river.

Lady Rosalind Fitzgerald was a tall woman, not pretty, but handsome in a stately way. She greeted the girls warmly, and said that Miss O'Connell had mentioned Deirdre's name to her.

When she took the piece of lace in her hands, however, she fell silent. The silence lasted so long that Deirdre began to grow terribly nervous. She had a feeling that Lady Rosalind was either looking for mistakes or trying to think of a way of saying that she did not want the lace without hurting Deirdre's feelings.

By the time Lady Rosalind did speak, Deirdre's hands were wet with sweat, and even Fiona was feeling rather worried.

'How old are you, Deirdre?' Lady Rosalind asked.

'I'm thirteen, my lady,' said Deirdre timidly.

Lady Rosalind drew in a deep breath. 'I can hardly believe it,' she said. 'This is the most wonderful piece of lace! Where did you get the pattern? I've never seen it before.'

'I designed it myself, my lady,' said Deirdre, with a little more confidence. 'Those are the ferns which grow around our cottage.'

'Well, Deirdre,' said Lady Rosalind decisively, 'I love your work. Will six pounds be enough for it? Hand me my purse from the table over there. Could you also hand me that silk parasol from behind that chair? I'd like you to take it home and make a lace cover for it.'

Deirdre found the purse and picked it up hesitantly. She had no idea what a parasol was, but Fiona – who had met the word in a book – picked up what Deirdre had thought of as a silk umbrella, and brought it over to Lady Rosalind.

Lady Rosalind looked at the tall blonde girl with interest.

'Thank you, my dear,' she said. 'Do you make lace as well?'

Fiona shook her head with a smile. 'No, my lady,' she said. 'I'm not good with my hands.'

'My sister writes stories,' said Deirdre bravely. 'Like Mr Charles Dickens does.'

'Really!'

Fiona could see that Lady Rosalind was highly amused and had turned away to hide a smile. I wish Deirdre hadn't said that, she thought, her whole face turning pink with embarrassment.

Lady Rosalind with a kind woman, and she was sorry that she had embarrassed the girl.

'Would you like to tell me about your stories, my dear?' she said. 'I want your sister to mend a lace overskirt for me, if she will be so kind. While she's doing that, I'll show you my library. I have five of Mr Dicken's books there. We'll go and look at them now; and when you're finished, Deirdre, I'll tell Williams to take you both back in the trap.'

When Lady Rosalind and Fiona came back from the library, Deirdre was relieved to see that her sister was looking happy and enthusiastic. Lady Rosalind praised Deirdre's neat mending of the overskirt and asked her to deliver the parasol, with its lace cover, in a few months' time.

'It's no use bringing it any earlier,' she said. 'I'm going to London shortly. Now I shall ring for Williams, so you'll have a nice ride home and not have to walk in all this heat.'

Deirdre did not like to ask Fiona any questions while they were in the trap with Williams, so it was only when they were walking up the avenue to the cottage that she heard what had happened. Lady Rosalind had asked Fiona to read to her; then she had talked to her about school, and Fiona had told her that her father had wanted her to be a teacher. Lady Rosalind had been enthusiastic about that idea. She had been so friendly that just before leaving the library, Fiona had found the courage to take her stories out of her basket and ask Lady Rosalind whether she would read them sometime.

'And she said she'd read them very carefully and let me know exactly what she thought, and that I shouldn't be discouraged if they're not too good, because most writers write quite a few stories before they have something good enough to publish,' finished Fiona, just as Daniel and Martin came running down the avenue to meet them.

'I've got four beautiful trout ready for dinner,' Daniel was shouting. 'Did you get five pounds, Deirdre?'

'No,' Deirdre called back.

'Oh . . . ' Daniel's face fell. He had been looking forward to buying a pony.

Deirdre could not bear to tease him for long; she added quickly, 'Better yet – I got six pounds!'

'Six pounds!' Martin said. 'I don't believe it. Show me.'

Without a word, Deirdre put her hand in her pocket and took out the six pounds. Martin's face lit up.

'Now we can buy some winter oats, as well,' he said joyfully. 'And you'll need to buy yourself some sewing things, Deirdre. We'll have a great day shopping on Saturday!'

'I suppose we won't have any money for things like gingerbread,' said Daniel, his voice light and careless, but his face wistful. He was remembering the time, before the famine, when they had gone to the fair at Ennis; John McMahon had bought pretty ribbons for the girls and tin whistles for Daniel and Martin, and everyone had had a piece of hot ginerbread.

'Don't be stupid,' Martin said roughly, and walked off. Daniel, rather crestfallen, followed him.

Fiona watched him sympathetically. She knew how he felt. If only they could go back a few years and have everything the way it used to be . . .

'I suppose there's no chance of having a few pennies left over to buy him a piece of gingerbread?' she said tentatively to Deirdre, as they went into the house. 'It's a shame, really; he's only twelve, and he doesn't have much fun. At least I have my stories and you have your lacemaking and Martin has the farm, but Daniel is always just doing jobs for everyone.'

All through dinner, Deirdre was thinking hard. Afterwards, when the two boys had gone to do the milking, she explained her idea to Fiona.

'You see,' she said, 'I've got lots of little pieces of net and cambric left over. If you help me, I could spend tomorrow and the next day making a whole lot of ribbons to see at the fair. They needn't cost much, and people like to have something cheap to spend their money on. We'll spend whatever money we earn from them on little treats for ourselves.'

So for the next two days Fiona snipped and basted, and Deirdre sewed. By Friday evening they had a basket of pretty lace ribbons, a few lace handkerchiefs, and some lovely collars, all made from the waste scraps in Deirdre's sewing basket.

They all went to bed early that night: they had to get up at six in the morning, milk the goats, feed the hens and the ducks, and then set out on the fifteen-mile walk to Ennis.

Chapter Twelve

That Saturday all Ennis market was a day which they would all remember vividly in the months to come. They arrived early; a farmer and his wife had picked them up along the way. Martin and Daniel went off to see about the pony, and Deirdre and Fiona nervously picked a good position, near the abbey, and displayed their ribbons.

For a while no one noticed them. Deirdre was beginning to despair. Fiona, however, was determined that they were going to see the ribbons. She started to walk around the crowd, with her basket on her arm; and within a few minutes, a long queue of girls formed, all wanting a lace ribbon.

By ten o'clock, all the ribbons had been sold and only one lace collar remained. It was the prettiest of all, and Deirdre hoped to get sixpence for it. Fiona took it over to the place where the judging of the prize heifers was going on. She watched while the winner was declared, and waited until the owner had been congratulated by all his friends; then, just as they were all making for the nearest public house, she walked up to him and put on her best smile.

'Would you like a lace collar for your wife?' she asked timidly, praying that he did have a wife.

'How much is it?' the farmer asked with a laugh.

'Only sixpence,' said Fiona, wondering whether she should ask for more in case he wanted to bargain. However, she need not have worried: the farmer put his hand in his pocket and handed her a sixpenny piece. Fiona thanked him and turned away, but he called after her and handed her two extra pennies.

'That's for yourself, girleen,' he said. 'Your mammy makes nice lace. Come on, lads, let's have a few drinks! I don't need to hurry now – I'll get a good welcome when I meet the missus with this in my pocket.'

Fiona returned to Deirdre in triumph. They counted up their money and were thrilled to find that they had six shillings. That would give Martin enough for some seed, if he needed to spend the whole six pounds on the pony, and they would still have enough for a few treats.

They wandered around the stalls, looking at the brightly-coloured things for sale. It was amazing: the roads were full of people dying of the famine, and yet there were enough well-off people around to buy and sell at the market.

Fiona bought some new copybooks for her stories, and Deirdre had a little brass thimble, to save her fingers from being pricked; they bought fishing lines and hooks for Daniel and Martin; and they bought four pieces of gingerbread.

Deirdre was just saying 'Let's go and find Martin,' when a voice from behind them said: 'That's the girl, Ma'am. That's the one who sold me the lace collar.'

Deirdre and Fiona turned in surprise. Behind them was the farmer who had bought the collar, and his wife, and with them was another woman – a short, fat woman with cold grey eyes, dressed in a long woollen cloak. It was the Matron of the Ennistymon workhouse.

'I thought so!' she said triumphantly. 'Those girls stole that lace from the workhouse. Help me to get them into my cart, over there; I must take them both back to Ennistymon with me.'

The farmer looked a little uneasy, glancing from Matron to the two white-faced girls before him. Deirdre was paralysed and speechless; but Fiona faced the woman boldly.

'We've never seen you before in our lives,' she said without hesitation.

'Don't tell lies, Fiona!' screamed Matron, her voice rising to a shrill screech which began to draw a crowd of onlookers. Farmers left the ring around the bullocks and came to see what was happening.

'What's wrong?' someone asked.

'This woman is the Matron of the Ennistymon workhouse,' explained the farmer, who was looking more and more embarrassed. 'She says the girls stole lace from her.'

'Ennistymon workhouse?' shouted another man. 'They starve people in that place. An old uncle of mine went in there, and he was dead in a fortnight; and when I saw him in his coffin, he was nothing but skin and bone.'

An ugly murmur began to rise from the growing crowd. Fiona looked around, with hope dawning in her eyes.

Then, to her horror, she caught sight of a policeman in the distance. Matron had not seen him yet, but once she did, it would all be over: he would break up the crowd and help her to drag the girls back to the workhouse.

As Fiona looked wildly around for some way to escape, her eye fell on a man who looked somehow familiar: a tall, burly fellow with a weathered brown face. Suddenly Fiona realised who it was: it was Mr Arkins, their neighbour of long ago.

Another farmer had been explaining the situation to him. Mr Arkins stroke into the centre of the crowd, towering over Matron, waving his heavy stick threateningly.

'Be off with you!' she shouted. 'What are you bothering my daughters for? Mary, Nellie, come on – come away from this madwoman! Your mother's over here. And you, woman – be off!'

Matron shrank back from the menace in his voice. All around, the crowd were muttering threats and curses, pressing in on her . . . Without another word, she turned and fled.

Fiona seized Deirdre's hand and followed Mr Arkins in the opposite direction.

'I wouldn't have known you – you've got so big, the pair of you – if it wasn't for meeting Martin and Daniel a while back,' he told them. 'Martin is the image of your father, God have mercy on him. That's how I knew him.'

Deirdre found her tongue. 'We're so grateful to you, Mr Arkins,' she said. 'I don't know what we'd have done if you hadn't come along.'

'Well, it would be a strange thing if I did nothing to help my neighbours' children – especially after all that your mother, God rest her, did for me and my family.'

'Where are you living now, Mr Arkins?' asked Fiona. She did not want to talk about her mother. Someday, perhaps, but not now.

'I'm living with my brother near Ennis, and the missus and all the children are there too,' he said. 'My brother is a bachelor, so we're just about managing. Look, I must get back to the ring; I'm selling a bullock for my brother. You'll be all right now, won't you? That old witch has got back into her cart, and she's off before they throw her in the pond. Work-house matrons aren't very popular around here. She won't be back in a hurry. – Look, there's Martin and Daniel over there. Looks like they've got themselves a fine Connemara pony.'

With a cheery wave, Mr Arkins was off, and Deirdre and Fiona pushed through the crowd to join their brothers.

Martin, for once, was beaming with excitement. The pony was beautiful: he was grey, with a broad back and sturdy legs and kind eyes, and he looked very strong. Martin had been forced to pay six pounds for him, so he was delighted when he heard of the success of the ribbon-selling.

When the twins told him about their lucky escape, however, Martin decided that they must leave immediately, just in case Matron decided to come back.

They bought a bag of Indian meal and hoisted it onto the pony's broad back. It was such a relief not to have to carry the bag that Martin was smiling to himself all the way down the road.

For the next two months the pony proved his worth on the farm. Gentle and good-tempered as he was, he was also immensely strong, and no amount of work tired him. He had been trained to the cart, and after Martin had driven him a few times Deirdre found that she could manage him on her own. She went for a few drives around Lough Fergus with Daniel; then, towards the end of July, she and Daniel went to Ennis to buy some new supplies. As Lady Rosalind Fitzgerald was not yet back from London, Deirdre tried to sell a few lace collars to the shop-keepers in Ennis, but she was offered such a poor price that she decided to keep them; if Lady Rosalind did not want them, Deirdre would bring Fiona with her the next time and let Fiona do the bargaining.

On the way home, Deirdre allowed Daniel to drive once they were outside Ennis. He had only gone a few miles when they saw a man and a woman plodding slowly along the raod to Corofin. Feeling very grown-up and pleased with himself, Daniel stopped and offered them a lift; but as the pair climbed wearily into the cart, Daniel went white.

The man's face was a dark yellow, and Daniel had seen that colour often enough in the workhouse to know what it meant. The man was suffering from yellow fever.

Daniel didn't know what to do. He and Deirdre wouldn't be able to turn the couple out of the cart. The man was still quite strong-looking – he was probably in the early stages of the sickness – and in any case, touching them and struggling with them would only spread the fever.

Daniel gave a worried look at Deirdre, who had noticed nothing. He and Martin had already had the yellow fever, when they were in the workhouse, and people said that once you had recovered from it you could not get it again; but neither Deirdre nor Fiona had ever had yellow fever. Deirdre was in deadly danger.

When they reached the next turn-off, Daniel stopped the cart.

'Deirdre,' he said,' could you get out and hold the horse's head? We turn off here,' he told the couple, ignoring Deirdre's startled face, 'so you'll have to get out now. Our parents wouldn't like to see strangers in the cart.'

For a moment he thought the man would refuse to get out; but then, in the distance, they heard the clip-clop of another horse and cart coming down the dusty road. The man shrugged his shoulders and climbed down, helped by his wife.

Deirdre suddenly realised how sick the man was. She stayed well away from him, holding the pony's head, feeling cold with horror. When she climbed back into the cart, she was careful not to touch anything that the man had touched.

Daniel turned down the side road and went on until they reached a well. There he stopped; taking a bucket from the cart, he filled it with clean water and poured bucketful after bucketful over the back of the cart.

'I don't know whether it will do any good or not,' he said finally. 'but at least we've done our best. Oh, don't get that yellow fever, Deirdre! It's horrible.'

'I'll do my best not to,' said Deirdre, with a shaky laugh. 'Don't let's tell the other two about this. There's no point in them worrying. Let's rub some of that wild garlic on our faces and hands. It's supposed to be good for keeping away fevers.'

For the whole of the next week, Daniel watched Deirdre with a sick feeling in his stomach. He was so worried that he found it hard to eat, and he started to have nightmares again. Night after night, they were all woken up by screams from the boys' room.

On Friday Fiona told Martin to take Daniel out for a day's fishing in Lake Lickeen.

'You haven't really used your fishing lines yet,' she said, 'so you might as well. There isn't too much to do around the farm, and it might cheer Daniel up. I don't know what's the matter with him. Deirdre is a bit down, too. She doesn't seem to be enjoying the lacemaking as much as she used to. I'll try to get her to go for a walk with me later on.'

Martin looked across at Deirdre. She was, as usual, hard at work, sitting at her outdoor table in the shade of the sycamore tree and sewing industriously. She looked the same as usual to him.

So when he and Daniel returned from their day's fishing, their bags full of fat trout, it came as a terrible shock to them to be met at the gate by Fiona, her face as white as Deirdre's lace and her brown eyes wide and transfixed with shock.

'It's Deirdre,' she said. 'She's locked the cottage door and she won't let me in. She says she's sick.

Chapter Thirteen

It's no wonder Daniel has been having night-mares, thought Fiona. It's almost as if he looked into the future, and saw that it was a mirror of the past. Everything was just as it had been during those terrible days when their mother lay dying. Martin had taken their father's place; he insisted that Fiona should keep out of the cottage and away from Deirdre.

'You'll have to sleep in the storeroom,' he said. 'Daniel and I will look after Deirdre. You can do some of Daniel's jobs around the farm, and he can do the cooking. Keep out in the air as much as possible. There's a good chance you won't get the fever.'

As the week went on, Deirdre grew sicker and sicker. At Fiona's suggestion, Martin tried to feed her honey in hot milk, but Deirdre was unable to keep any of it down. The continual vomiting was weakening her terribly; Martin feared that if she did not improve soon, she would be dead by the end of the week.

And the three of them had a new worry as well. The bag of Indian meal was nearly finished, and neither the oats nor the potatoes were ready for harvesting. Fiona scoured the countryside for herbs, and they had their own cabbages, but that would not be enough for healthy appetites when the Indian meal was finished.

Thank God for the eggs and the honey, thought Fiona. There was no money to buy more meal; they had all been so sure that Deirdre could earn as much as they needed that they had spent their last penny.

However, Fiona could not worry too much about money. The twins, so different in every way, were linked by an almost physical bond, and Fiona felt Deirdre's sickness almost as if it were her own. She did all her tasks mechanically – milking the goats, feeding the hens, collecting the eggs, fetching water from the well – but all the time she felt blank and empty. Even her beloved stories were of no consolation to her. For the first time in her life, she was unable to lose herself in her imaginary world. She walked around the farm with

Spooky in her arms, but not even Spooky could comfort her.

She kept trying to cheer herself up with the memory that Daniel and Martin had both begun to improve a little after a week. Surely Deirdre would do the same! Fiona eagerly counted off the days.

Friday came, and then Saturday, and still Daniel's report was the same: Deirdre was no better. The day dragged past. When Fiona brought the milk to the door in the evening, she only looked a question; and Daniel just shook his head.

Blinded by tears, Fiona turned and walked down the avenue. It had been a lovely day, a beautiful day in the middle of a beautiful summer, and Fiona could still feel the evening sun warm on her back. She was going down to meet Martin, who had been weeding the potatoes in the Big Meadow, but she knew that she would get no comfort from him. He was under great strain, and when Martin was under strain he didn't want to talk to anyone.

Still, Fiona decided that anything was better than keeping her terrors to herself. She continued around the bend in the avenue. Then she stopped abruptly.

Martin was at the gate, and he was not alone. A short, thick-set man was facing him, holding a horse and speaking loudly in a strange, almost incomprehensible accent. Fiona could not understand what he was saying, but she could see Martin's knuckles whiten as he gripped the gate. Under his tan, her brother's face had gone a queer yellowish-grey.

'One week, then. No longer,' said the stranger, climbing back onto his horse. He held up his left hand and two fingers of his right, speaking slowly and distinctly, each word separate. 'understand . . . Paddy? . . . Seven . . . days.'

Martin said nothing, just walked through the gate and closed it behind him. Fiona could bear the suspense no longer; as the strange rode off, she cried out, 'Oh, Martin, what is it? What's wrong?'

Martin hesitated and took a deep breath. He was a boy and he was fourteen years old. He couldn't be going to cry. He clenched his hands so tightly that the nails bit into his work-toughened palms. Then with a great effort, he answered as calmly as he could: 'The farm had been bought from something called the Encumbered Estates. It's been bought by an Englishman, and that was his agent. He says we owe him a year's rent. We must pay him five pounds by next Friday or we'll be evicted, thrown out. It'll be the workhouse again, I suppose.'

As soon as he said it, Martin's hard-won composure broke. He thought of the months of hard work, of how well the farm was coming along, of the potatoes growing strong and healthy, of how they had slaved and hoped and contrived – and it was all to end in this. He sat down on the grass beside the avenue and buried his face in his knees, and his shoulders shook with sobs.

Fiona knelt beside him, her arms around him, crying to keep him company. The sun grew lower in the sky and the shadows from the fuchsia bushes lengthened, but still they sat there – until the ducks, indignant at not being put in their house, came marching down the avenue and stood in a row, turning their heads from side to side, staring at Martin and Fiona, first with one small round eye and then with the other.

There was something so comic about them that Fiona could not help giving a slightly hysterical giggle. With an effort, Martin wiped his eyes and steadied his voice.

'If only Deirdre were well enough to work,' he said. 'Or if I'd had the sense not to buy the pony. If I sell him now, I'll probably only get a few pounds. I think I paid too much for him in the first place. People will always cheat a boy . . . We can never lay our hands on five pounds. He knows that. He just wants to get rid of us.'

Fiona said nothing. For the first time in her life, she could think of nothing to say.

Martin got to his feet, wiping the pieces of grass from his trousers.

'I'll say nothing to Daniel tonight,' he said in a flat, dead voice, as he set off up the avenue. 'You'd better go to bed when you've shut up the ducks.'

Fiona watched him go. His shadow, on the stony ground of the avenue, looked strange. It was the shape of an old man, she thought, a hunched-up old man. She could not bear to follow him – to walk past the cottage and see the clean limewashed walls, the familiar red door, the neatly-swept yard.

She turned and went through the fuchsia bushes into the Togher Field. She climbed the hill, seeing the soft pinks and crimsons of the western sky ahead of her and knowing that the next day would be another perfect summer day. She went into the fort, pulled aside the slab and climbed down into the underground storeroom. She threw herself, fully-dressed, on top of her hay-bag, and cried herself to sleep.

It was the middle of the night when something woke Fiona. She sat up abruptly, but could not think what that strange, high pitched shriek could have been. She listened, her hands cold, and heard the shriek again.

She knew what it was. There was a fox out there, probably a vixen teaching her cubs to hunt.

And I left the ducks out! realised Fiona, in horror. The poor little ducks! They were so stupid – they were probably still standing around the avenue waiting for her. At the thought of Spooky, her darling nervous little duck, being attacked by a fox, Fiona knew she would have to do something. She felt around in the darkness until she found the tinderbox and the storm lantern. She struck a light and lit the storm lantern, carefully closing its little door, and climbed out of the underground room.

When she came out, she realised that she did not really need the lantern. The full moon had risen and there were no clouds in the sky; it was as bright as day. Fiona decided to leave the lantern behind – for some reason the ducks were frightened of lanterns – so she put it down inside the passageway to the storeroom. She made her way out of the fort, passed the little cottage shining white in the moonlight, and went down the avenue.

There was no further sound from the fox. Foxes were clever; they had probably smelt Fiona coming and fled back across the river to the O'Donoghues' land. Spooky came flying up to meet her mistress, and the other ducks waddled behind as Fiona carried Spooky up to their cabin. As soon as he opened the door, they crowded in, jostling one another in their eagerness to be safely inside.

Fiona locked the door and turned back towards the cottage. She was conscious of a feeling of irritation with herself. My sister is dying, she thought, my brother is in the last stages of despair, we are going to lose our home again, and I go worrying about ducks. Still, she couldn't help being glad that she had saved them from the fox.

She stood outside the cottage for a moment. She knew that Deirdre was in the east room, the room which had once been their parents'. Walking quietly, Fiona went around to the front of the house. The moon shone into the little room, and Fiona could see Deirdre lying there, her eyes shut, her hair damp and matted around her white face. She was so still and so white that for a moment Fiona thought her sister was dead; but then a spasm of pain crossed Deirdre's face and her fist clenched.

For a long time Fiona stood there, tears running down her face, watching her sister, unable to do anything to help her. Finally she turned away and climbed up the hill into the fort.

The lantern was still where she had left it; she brought it down the steep steps and sat down on her bed. She was not sleepy, and she could not bear to blow out the little light, so she sat there holding the lantern and moving its comforting light around the stone walls.

I never really noticed the walls before, she thought. It's funny the way three of them are made of squared stones and the fourth is just rough boulders piled on top of each other . . . Fiona went over to the rough wall, holding the lantern high to look at the way that the irregular shapes had been fitted together. There did not seem to be any real mortar holding the stones, but sticky grey clay from the fields had been packed into the gaps. Fiona idly scratched at the dried clay. A lump of it fell out, and the lantern-light caught a flash of gold in the wall.

Fiona frowned in puzzlement. She held the lantern as near to the wall as possible: there was definitely a gleam of gold.

Trembling with excitement, she put down the lantern and scraped at the hard dry clay with her fingernails.

Another lump came away, and Fiona's fingers touched something hard and smooth, much too smooth to be stone. She picked up the lantern again and looked at the object she had uncovered.

It was a necklace, and it was the most beautiful thing Fiona had ever seen. It was made of two delicate ribbons of gold, twisted together; on one end was a small loop, on the other an elaborately-ornamented hook. Fiona held the necklace in her hand and looked at it with awe. She doubted whether even Lady Rosalind Fitzgerald owed such a marvellous necklace.

Without stopping to think, she scrambled up the steep passageway and went flying out of the fort, down the hill towards the cottage.

'Martin! Martin!' she screamed, bursting into the kitchen. 'Martin, look what I've found!'

Still half asleep, Martin came out of the boys' room, frowning angrily at the sight of Fiona.

'What are you doing here?' he asked crossly.

Fiona ignored his tone.

'Look, Martin,' she repeated, holding out the necklace. 'Look at what I found in the storeroom!'

Martin stretched out his hand and took the necklace from her. He stirred up the lumps of turf in the fireplace, but the heap of soft brown ash gave only a faint glow, so he went to the open door and held the necklace up to the white light of the moon. Daniel joined Fiona and they stood silently, hand in hand, while Martin turned the necklace over and over between his fingers.

'Is it gold?' whispered Fiona at last, unable to bear the suspense any longer.

Martin did not answer; he put the end of the necklace between his teeth and bit it gently.

'I . . . I think it is,' he stammered. 'It looks like gold, and it's soft – Da once told me that the way to test gold is to bite it and see if your teeth leave marks. I can hardly believe it, but I think it is gold.'

'Gold!' shrieked Daniel, unable to control himself any longer.

'Shh,' whispered Fiona and Martin together, suddenly remembering their sick sister; but it was too late. A weak voice was calling from the east room.

'Martin, could you bring me a drink of milk?'

Martin opened the door, signalling to Fiona to keep back.

'I'll heat some up for you in a minute, Deirdre. I need to poke up the fire a bit. How do you feel?'

And then the night which had begun in such agony ended in a blaze of excitement and hope. Deirdre said, in a voice which was beginning to sound stronger, 'I think I feel a little better. Would you bring me a piece of bread and some honey? I'm hungry.'

Chapter Fourteen

The next morning Deirdre had definitely improved. She was sitting up and eating a little food. Martin decided that she was well enough to be left in Daniel's care, so he harnessed up the pony and cart, and he and Fiona set off for Ennis to sell the gold necklace.

During the fifteen-mile drive to Ennis, Martin and Fiona hardly spoke. Everything depended on how much the gold necklace could be sold for. If only they could get five pounds for it, they could pay the rent and manage for food until Deirdre was well enough to work again.

When they reached Ennis, they tied the pony to a post and went into the pawnbroker's shop. There was a middle-aged countryman there, a simple kindly-looking man, and he had a ten-pound note in his hand.

'Will you give me two pounds for this?' he was asking the pawnbroker. Fiona saw the pawnbroker's face light up with greed. She supposed that he was used to country people not having much idea of the value of money, but this was too much for him. Visibly trying to control a desire to laugh, he rapidly wrote out a pawn ticket and handed it to the man with a flourish.

'There you are, my good man,' he said condescendingly. 'Your note will be safe as houses, here in my drawer, until you come to redeem it.'

Martin and Fiona looked at the countryman in astonishment. He seemed quite happy. They followed him out of the shop, and Martin said hesitantly, 'Excuse me, sir, but do you know that the bank would give you ten pounds for that note?'

The man was not offended; he smiled kindly at Martin. 'I know that, son,' he said, 'but then the bank would keep my ten-pound note, and I don't want to lose it. I've had that note since the night of the Big Wind. Do you remember it? It was about eight years ago. I found the ten-pound note in a ditch the day after.'

Martin nodded. He did remember the night of the Big Wind. He had been six years old. Their own thatch had blown off, and he remembered his father saying that lots of people in the parish had lost their savings that night – the thatch was always the place where country people were inclined to put anything that they wanted to keep hidden.

'Yes, but . . .' he said, feeling rather confused. However, the man was quite happy with the deal he had struck with the pawnbroker; with a friendly smile at them both, he walked down the street with his two pounds in his pocket and his ten-pound note in the pawnbroker's drawer.

'Well!' said Fiona. 'Don't let's try that pawnbroker, Martin. He'll be bound to cheat us, just like he cheated that poor man. Let's try that jeweller's shop across the road.

The jeweller's shop was the most magnificent place they had ever seen: diamonds and silver and gold gleamed from every side, and the floor was covered in a moss-green carpet. It was the first time Martin had ever seen a carpet, and he thought walking on it felt like walking on wet sand. He felt unable to speak in this palace of a shop. He took the necklace out of his pocket and handed it silently to Fiona.

The shop was very quiet, after the noise and bustle outside. There were two jewellers: one was in a corner, showing some jewellery to a fashionably-dressed lady, and the other was polishing some silver watches. Fiona walked up to him and said in her best English: 'Could you tell me how much this necklace is worth, please?'

The jeweller looked disdainfully at the shabby boy and girl and gave a careless glance at the necklace. What he saw in Fiona's hand, however, made his glance sharpen. He took the necklace from her abruptly and carried it over to the lamp. He screwed a little eyeglass into his eye socket and spent a long time examining it.

Fiona found herself getting quite excited. Surely, she thought, he wouldn't spend so long on the necklace if it were worth nothing! She clenched her hands tightly, willing him to say 'five pounds' as he came back to the counter. But the jeweller said nothing; he took a small glass with a handle from a drawer, went back to the necklace, and carried on examining it.

Eventually he beckoned to Martin and Fiona. They crossed the carpeted floor and stood beside him.

'Where did you get this necklace?' he asked in a low voice.

'I found it in a storeroom on our farm,' said Fiona.

The man gave her a suspicious look. 'You mean you stole it,' he said roughly.

'No, I didn't,' said Fiona, her voice reduced to a mere whisper by alarm.

Martin came to himself at that. 'Don't speak to my sister like that,' he said. 'It's none of your business, anyway. Just tell us how much you'll give for it.'

The man gave a careless shrug. 'Well, a pound,' he said. 'Or maybe two,' he added, seeing the look of disbelief on Martin's face.

'Two pounds!' Fiona's voice was high and loud with despair. Two pounds was no good to them. They had to have five pounds. She picked up the necklace. Could it be true that such a beautiful thing was only worth two pounds?

Martin saw the fashionable lady in the corner look up from the jewellery and glance across with interest.

To her surprise, she crossed the room and touched Fiona on the shoulder.

'So it is you, Fiona,' said Lady Rosalind Fitzgerald. 'I thought it sounded like your voice. What have you got here?' She bent over and examined the necklace carefully, then laid it down and looked at the jeweller.

'Well, really, Mr Smith,' she said icily, 'either I don't know much about jewellery or you don't. I would have thought that this necklace would be worth at least ten pounds, not two pounds. It is obviously an antique and of the most beautiful workmanship.'

'Well, my lady,' stammered the jeweller, but Lady Rosalind interrupted him.

'I don't think you should sell this necklace for two pounds, Fiona. Do you want money for a particular purpose? You know I'll pay Deirdre for the lace parasol-cover when she brings it to me. Come outside and tell me all about it.'

Without another glance at the embarrassed jeweller, Lady Rosalind swept out of the shop. Fiona snatched up the necklace and followed her.

Lady Rosalind's carriage was outside the shop. Fiona and Martin got in and told her how they needed five pounds for the rent, and how they had found the necklace. Lady Rosalind thought for a moment and then said decisively: 'I will lend you the money for the rent. It would be very sad if this necklace were sold, even for its full worth. It must have belonged to one of your family, and it should stay in your family. You can pay me back whenever you have some spare money. My agent tells me that he thinks it might be a good year for potatoes and other crops, after this lovely summer; and Deirdre will soon be able to earn plenty of money with her lacemaking.'

She opened her purse and offered Martin a five-pound note; but he shook his head. Fiona watched him anxiously. Surely he couldn't refuse!

Martin, however, knew exactly what he wanted to do. He took the necklace from Fiona and handed it to Lady Rosalind. 'I'll only take the money,' he said, 'if you'll take the necklace.'

Lady Rosalind looked at him and realised that his pride would not let him take the money as a present. 'I'll keep the necklace, then,' she said. 'I'll keep it safe until you pay me back.'

Martin's face lightened, and he gratefully took the five-pound note. He tried to thank Lady Rosalind, but she would have none of it.

'That is a most beautiful necklace,' she said. 'It's beautiful enough to be worn at Queen Victoria's court. I wish I'd had it last week. However, I'm going to a ball tomorrow at Dromoland Castle. May I wear it then? I'll take good care of it for you.'

'A ball!' Fiona's eyes lit up with excitement. I wish I could go to a ball, she thought. What a wonderful story I could make out of it!

Lady Rosalind looked at her and smiled at the thought of the pleasure she was about to give her.

'By the way, Fiona,' she said, 'I owe you some money.'

She opened her purse again; this time she took out a gold guinea and gave it to Fiona.

Fiona looked at it in bewilderment.

'I don't understand,' she said. 'Why would you owe me money, my lady?'

Lady Rosalind smiled. 'Well, I sold something you gave me,' she said. 'Do you remember what you gave me before I went to London?'

'My stories,' said Fiona in a whisper.

'Yes, your stories. I read them all and I liked them all, but the one I thought was best – the one that showed that you could grow up to be a writer – was the one called "Old Sally".'

Fiona was silent. She turned the golden guinea over and over in her hands, trying to take in the good news. So perhaps someday she would be a writer!

In a way she was half-disappointed at the story Lady Rosalind had chosen, because it was almost a true story. She had started it in her mind the night after Old Sally had died, when she had been thinking about her and trying to imagine what Old Sally had been like as a young girl, and she had told the whole truth about the workhouse.

Lady Rosalind broke the silence. 'I have something else for you, too, Fiona,' she said, 'but you'll have to come to the house to collect it. It's a letter from Mr Charles Dickens. He's the editor of the magazine which is going to publish your story. Mr Dickens is always very kind to young writers, and he has some advice for you.'

'I can't believe it,' Fiona said. 'I feel as if I'm in the middle of a dream.'

'Well, come and see me when Deirdre is better. And remember, I'm just borrowing that necklace for a while. It belongs to Drumshee and it must stay in Drumshee.'

After they had left Lady Rosalind, Fiona and Martin did not want to stay in Ennis any longer. Fiona wanted to make sure that Deirdre was well, and Martin could not bear to wait one unnecessary minute before putting the rent in the agent's hands and making sure that the farm was safe.

As they clattered along the road to Corofin, Martin at last broke the silence.

'Do you know,' he said quietly, 'for the first time since Ma and Da died, I feel as if I can see a future.'

Fiona drew a deep breath. She, too, could see a future at last. She held firmly on to the rough wooden seat of the jolting cart and imagined it. Deirdre, well and strong again, growing rich with her lacemaking business – perhaps even moving to London to join Miss O'Connell . . . Martin, so like his father in every way, would be a farmer and farm Drumshee. Fiona looked at him with affection, imagining the sort of man he would be: never a great talker, but honest, straightforward and courageous. Perhaps someday one of his sons might own Drumshee, and the family would no longer have to live in fear of the landlord . . .

And what about Daniel? The farm was not big enough for two families. Perhaps Daniel would emigrate – he might go to America, or even to Australia. Fiona remembered how he had loved it when she read him a story from the Sixth Reader, about Australia and the great discoveries of Captain Cook . . .

And me? thought Fiona. Where will I be?

Slowly a picture grew in her mind – a picture of herself going back to school, studying hard, gradually learning enough to become a teacher; and writing all the while, every night, writing better and better stories, getting more and more of them published, until at last she was a real writer whose books were read all over the country. Perhaps she too would go to England, to London, and meet Charles Dickens and all the great writers . . .

But the cart was turning in at the gate of Drumshee, and there was Daniel running down the avenue; and best of all, there was Deirdre at the cottage door – weak and pale, but smiling joyfully as Martin jumped down from the cart and waved the five pounds in front of her.

Fiona shook her hair back from her face with a smile. I don't need to daydream about the future, she thought. The present is enough.

She tossed the reins to Daniel, leaped down after Martin and ran to hug Deirdre. The family had been saved – saved by the ancient secret of Drumshee.

Also from WOLFHOUND PRESS . . .

BOOK 13 in the Drumshee Timeline Series

Secret Spy
from
Drumshee

It's 1828 and election fever has hit Drumshee. Daniel O'Connell is trying to get elected as the first Catholic Member of Parliament ever. He wants to help Ireland's Catholics – but some people want to stop him and they're ready to kill him if they have to.

The twins from Drumshee, Mary Ann and Ronan, vow to protect Daniel O'Connell. Mary Ann uses her charm to get information and Ronan makes the perfect secret spy – he's so quiet nobody suspects him.

Election Day is getting nearer and the tension is building. Will Ronan spot an assassin in time? And if he does, how will he save Daniel O'Connell?

COMING SOON . . .

BOOK 14 in the Drumshee Timeline Series

Banished
from
Drumshee

'And I took his body in my arms, and I carried him up to the top of Mount Callan.

And I laid him in the shallow grave that I had hollowed out of the stony soil.

And then I shovelled the earth over him and hid him forever.'

I carried over a heavy flagstone and placed it on the mound.

And with my knife I carved these words.

'Here lies Conan, the fierce and turbulent.'

Who was Conan? Why was he called 'fierce and turbulent'? How did he die? Who buried him?

In the Eigth Century turmoil of warring tribes, love, jealousy, blackmail and revenge, Conan's story unfolds. He entangles his foster brother, Columba, and the beautiful Sorcha in a terrifying adventure that will change all their lives forever.

★ ★ ★

Orders or Enquiries to:
Wolfhound Press
An Imprint of Merlin Publishing
16 Upper Pembroke Street, Dublin 2, Ireland
publishing@merlin.ie
www.merlin-publishing.com